Tainted Glory
in Handel's
Messiah

Tainted Glory in Handel's *Messiah*

The Unsettling History of the
World's Most Beloved Choral Work

MICHAEL MARISSEN

Yale
UNIVERSITY PRESS
New Haven & London

Published with assistance from the Annie Burr Lewis Fund and from the foundation established in memory of Calvin Chapin of the Class of 1788, Yale College.

Yale University Press books may be purchased in quantity for educational, business, or promotional use. For information, please e-mail sales.press@yale.edu (U.S. office) or sales@yaleup.co.uk (U.K. office).

Designed by Newgen North America
Set in Sabon type by Newgen
Printed in the United States of America

Library of Congress Cataloging-in-Publication Data

Marissen, Michael.
Tainted glory in Handel's *Messiah* : the unsettling history of the world's most beloved choral work / Michael Marissen.
pages cm
Includes bibliographical references and index.
ISBN 978-0-300-19458-6 (hardcover : alk. paper)
1. Handel, George Frideric, 1685–1759. Messiah.
2. Antisemitism in music.   I. Title.
ML410.H13M38 2014
782.23—dc23
2013034526

A catalogue record for this book is available from the British Library.

This paper meets the requirements of
ANSI/NISO Z39.48-1992 (Permanence of Paper).

10 9 8 7 6 5 4 3 2 1

Frontispiece: Erfurt Cathedral, Foolish Virgins with abject Synagoga. Kolossos / Wikimedia Commons. http://commons.wikimedia.org/wiki/File:Erfurt-Dom -rechtehaelfte-Seiteneingang.jpg.

for Lauren

You have heard, LORD, their contempt, all their designs against me. . . . Look! *I am their music.*

—Book of Lamentations 3:61,63b

But if some of the branches were broken and you, being a wild olive tree, were grafted in among them and became a joint sharer of the root of the richness of the olive tree, *do not rejoice against the branches.* . . . All Israel will be saved.

—Letter of Paul to the Romans 11:17–18a,26a

CONTENTS

ACKNOWLEDGMENTS

For generously granting access to their various rare materials, I am grateful to Robin A. Leaver and to a host of marvelous librarians: Peggy Seiden and Pam Harris at the McCabe Library of Swarthmore College, Emily Walhout at the Houghton Library of Harvard University, Michael Terry at the Dorot Jewish Division of the New York Public Library, Maria Isabel Molestina at the Morgan Library and Museum, Katharine Hogg and Colin Coleman at the Gerald Coke Handel Collection of the Foundling Hospital Museum in London, and Martin Wyatt at the Handel House Museum in London.

For criticism and encouragement I am most grateful to the brilliant students in the graduate seminar on religious polemic in the music of Bach and Handel that I taught for the spring semester 2010 at the University of Pennsylvania: Suzanne Bratt, Delia Casadei, Myron Gray, Stephan Hammel, Scott Ordway, and Emily Joy Rothchild.

I am also thankful for invitations to deliver lectures on the subject at Case Western Reserve University, City University of New York, the Julliard School, Lafayette College, Liverpool Hope University, Queen Mary–University of London, University of Leuven, University of Maryland, University of Minnesota, University of Oxford, Vanderbilt University, and elsewhere. Likewise, for being able to contribute a paper on the subject for a meeting of the American Handel Society at Princeton University; a meeting of the Bach Colloquium at Harvard University; a meeting of the Forum on Music and Christian Scholarship at Calvin College; and a national meeting of the American Musicological Society in Los Angeles.

My profound thanks to Lars Fischer and Ed Kessler for inviting me to be visiting fellow for the fall term 2012 at the Centre for the Study of Jewish-Christian Relations, Woolf Institute, Cambridge, United Kingdom, and for providing me with a marvelous atmosphere in which to complete this work. Likewise to the provost and colleagues at Swarthmore College for moral and financial support.

My deep appreciation goes to Eric Brandt, senior editor at Yale University Press, for his remarkable sensitivity and intelligence. My thanks also to Eric's superb editorial assistants, Niamh Cunningham and Erica Hanson, and to Jenya Weinreb, managing editor at the Press, and Mary Pasti, assistant managing editor. For eagle-eyed copyediting and proofreading, I thank Jay Harward, Newgen project manager and editor, and Jay's colleagues Katherine Faydash and Christine Gever.

For reading part or all of the typescript in its various earlier stages, my profound thanks likewise to Roger Bullard, Tony Godzieba, Dan Melamed, Barbara Milewski, Cal Stapert, Ray van Leeuwen, Al Wolters, and especially Awet Andemicael and Michael Rose (both of whom also provided me with several extremely useful formulations).

Above all, I thank Lauren Belfer. She knows the reasons why.

Tainted Glory
in Handel's
Messiah

I

INTRODUCTION

BRIEFLY, WHY I LOVE HANDEL

When I was a child in the 1960s and my Dutch Calvinist immigrant family bought our first record player, among the half dozen or so LPs we acquired was the classic recording of *Messiah* by Eugene Ormandy with the Mormon Tabernacle Choir and the Philadelphia Orchestra. My parochial school education had made me deeply familiar with the Bible, and therefore I recognized the scriptural texts used in Handel's masterpiece. But in those days I wasn't much interested in the words, and I more or less ignored them. What inspired me was the staggering magnificence of Handel's music.

For my youthful self, aesthetic contemplation was all that mattered. Each and every time the choir surged to "And his name shall be called: WON-der-ful, COUN-sel-lor, the Might-y GOD, the Ev-er-LAST-ing FA-ther, the PRINCE OF PEACE!" I felt an unspeakable tremor of excitement, and every time the soloist belted out "WHY do the NA-tions so FU-rious-ly rage to-GETH-er," an exquisite thrill. Not to mention the tremendous rush given by the big finish at "King of KINGS, and Lord of LORDS, Hal-le-LU-jah, Hal-le-LU-jah, Hal-le-LU-jah, Hal-le-LU-jah, Hal-LE- . . . lu-JAH!"

The sound of great music became my passion, and I eventually went on to get degrees in music history from Calvin College and Brandeis University. And now for more than twenty years I've had the great pleasure of teaching the subject at Swarthmore College.

My specialty as a teacher and scholar has always been music of the baroque period, and in time I did come to include the study of its religious aspects.

A few years ago, I was asked to write an essay about theological anti-Judaism in Handel's *Messiah* for the Easter Sunday issue of the *New York Times*.[1] Soon after its publication I received a large number of emails, most of them expressing either strongly positive or strongly negative reactions. A continual complaint among the negative responses was, essentially, "Anti-Judaism! Are you kidding me? You can't be right. What's *wrong* with you—why do you hate Handel so much?"

Perhaps such complaints ought simply to be dismissed as ad hominem arguments. But I do regret, very much, having needlessly alienated any of my audience, and so I want here at the outset of this study to speak to these readers' concerns.

Although my reading of *Messiah* as anti-Judaic may or may not be right, the truth is that I will always adore Handel.

Handel's music is simply in my blood, as I've countless times enjoyed performing his exquisite chamber music in concert, and I'm also constantly listening to CDs of his concertos, cantatas, operas, and oratorios. To me, this is some of the most life-enhancing art on the planet. Sticking just to *Messiah* for several specific examples, I continue to be transported by the harmonic buildup and release in the exuberant closing strains of the chorus "For unto us a Child is born"; likewise by the brilliant scaffolding of the fugue on the words "for the Lord God omnipotent reigneth" in the Hallelujah chorus; by the aching humanity expressed in the appoggiaturas at the words "He was wounded for our transgressions, He was bruised for our iniquities" in the chorus "Surely He hath born our griefs"; and by the fierce radiance of the choral block chords at the opening of "Worthy is the Lamb that was slain."

For me, *Messiah* is music of tremendous artistic and life-affirming spiritual beauty. There's no end of good and right reasons *Messiah* has become such a popular and beloved work. A comprehensive study of the oratorio would speak fully to this. This book, however, focuses on only one *aspect* of the work. I profoundly regret that this aspect is there to be exposed.

Here's the agonizing heart of the problem as I see and hear it: the magnificent joy of Handel's music is not merely at odds with a dreadful anti-Judaic message in *Messiah*; it is at the very same time a scandalous affirmation of that message. The ecstatic grace, the life-affirming levitation of the listening heart and mind, are all working in concert with a triumphal squashing of Jews. (So far as I can tell, the words and musical setting of *Messiah* do not in any way subvert their anti-Judaic message at the same time that they enunciate it.) Can such life-enhancing music possibly also be invested with life-defeating hatred?

It appears that it can.

ISSUES OF METHOD IN
INTERPRETATION OF MUSIC

Questions of method are always an issue in scholarly writing about the arts. And probably because music is a nonverbal and nonvisual medium, an art that is thus both so technical and so mysterious, writing about music has its own particular issues and challenges.

"Purely aesthetic" approaches—focusing on technical features—are still largely the normal practice in the academic field of music and are also accepted or expected by the general public. Over many years as a teacher and scholar, though, I—like many of my colleagues—have slowly become dissatisfied with appreciating music for its magnificence alone and with studying only the development of music's forms. These approaches can come to feel like somewhat hollow endeavors. I and my like-minded colleagues have increasingly wondered whether anyone could truly be said to understand great musical works if his or her knowledge were only formal and aesthetic.

In my lectures on music and meaning I often put forward the (imperfect) analogy of the "head turner." There are many people whose sole or primary interest in an amatory partner might generously be called "aesthetic." It's a free country, of course—but can people ever truly understand partners by contemplating only their looks, ignoring their thoughts, their feelings, their history, their points of view? I, for one, would respond with a strong and definitive no: the appreciation solely of pleasing appearance does not and cannot ever provide a full understanding of a person, or indeed of anything else.

I was later buoyed up in coming across the American philosopher Arthur Danto's most trenchant expression of this probable misunderstanding of art as only a thing of pleasure. He writes (my emphases): "Distinguishing the fine from the applied arts, and identifying the former as 'les beaux arts,' constitutes a form of repression masked as exaltation paralleled only by the perception of women as the Fair Sex. To put works of art or to set women at what came to be known as an 'aesthetic distance'—as objects whose essence and fulfillment consists in pleasing the senses—was a brilliant political response to what were felt as dark dangers in both [women and art.] . . . [In the arts,] aesthetic distance then does what frames and pedestals do to icons and effigies, isolating them conceptually from the practical world and humiliating them as objects fit only to caress the *disinterested* and *refined* eye."[2]

So, to adapt these critical ideas to *Messiah*, I will say that going with the conventional view that art is merely beautiful or magnificent may help us to experience great pleasure from Handel's masterpiece, but it doesn't help us much in understanding the work.

You might object, though, that you really don't wish to understand *Messiah*; you simply want to *enjoy* it—to revel in its means, not reflect on its aims. If that is so, you will want to forgo reading this book.

But if you are in fact interested also in understanding the likely aims of *Messiah*, the question is, how can you take stock of the piece in a way that brings proper understanding? In this case the words that Handel set to music play a central role.

Now, it's true that many great classical vocal works still hold people's attention today because of the musical setting alone, not because of the words. That is to say, we wouldn't even be talking about these pieces if not for the music. This is the case, many would agree, for example, with Mozart's opera *The Magic Flute*. The story of *The Magic Flute* may seem somewhat bird-brained, but Mozart's music soars.

My subject, however, isn't why or how Handel's *Messiah* is great music. Rather, it's what Handel's *Messiah* plausibly means. And in any event, I would argue that *Messiah*, a bit like Bach's *St. Matthew Passion* and *St. John Passion*, is a special case. *Messiah* has assumed a central place in the choral repertory largely, in fact, because of the words.

Most of my fellow Handel enthusiasts will tell you that Handel wrote equally good or even better music than *Messiah* (for example, his oratorio *Theodora*). What makes *Messiah* exceptional is its libretto. The librettist of *Messiah*, Handel's friend and colleague

Charles Jennens, didn't follow the usual practice of creating poetic paraphrases. Instead, he drew directly on the glorious language of the King James Version of the Bible, compiling complementary passages, more or less verbatim, from its Old and New Testament. In this way, Jennens's libretto lays out the basic beliefs of traditional Christianity.

Whether or not you're a Christian believer, once you've committed yourself to a close study of *Messiah*'s libretto, an important interpretive issue arises. How can you be certain about a text's range of plausible meanings?

For the purpose of organizing a close reading, teachers of literary criticism have long advocated several categories of inquiry. They speak of the three "worlds" of a text. The first category applies to the world inside the text. This concerns the inner workings of the text itself—that is to say, its wording, its structure and style, and the subject matter that it portrays. The second category focuses on the world behind the text. This refers to cultural background, to how the text was produced and how it originally functioned. And the third category considers the world in front of the text. This has to do with the text's opening up a figurative universe that can be inhabited by the reader.

The meanings, in the fullest sense, of a work emerge only when the world projected by the text interacts with the lifeworld of the reader's own assumptions and experiences: both the figurative world of the work and the real world of the reader affect and challenge each other in order to generate justified meaning.

In this short book I focus mostly on the worlds inside and behind Handel's *Messiah*, that is, on the exact words of the oratorio and on the milieu that produced them.

In my view, appraisal of *Messiah* has a tendency to overemphasize the lifeworld of the listener's own assumptions and experiences, effectively or even explicitly saying that the only thing that matters is "what it means to me, right now." This unmindfulness of history, this excessive presentism (that is, the notion that only present, unmediated experience counts in questions of meaning, without external demands, such as historical considerations, being placed on listeners), seems often to hold true for text-slighting aesthetes and text-esteeming Christian believers alike. Surely, however, classic artworks carry traces of past reference, as a sort of palimpsest, even if modern audiences can't perceive them unaided. While I don't wish to underrate the value of direct present-day experience of *Messiah*, I do see great worth in helping interested listeners to be more historically informed.

Furthermore, when Jennens compiled his passages of Scripture for *Messiah*, he assumed its listeners would be fairly familiar with the Bible. In some places the sense of Jennens's libretto is practically incomprehensible without that broader knowledge. I also see great benefit, then, in helping interested listeners to become better biblically informed.

Once you start to look carefully at how Jennens placed his biblical passages next to one another, and once you consider the various historical sources and contexts for his decisions, you'll see an issue that hasn't been probed in previous books on *Messiah*. At the time the piece was written, and indeed for some time afterward (including, in some circles, to this day), several of *Messiah*'s key biblical passages were straightforwardly understood, and indeed welcomed, in part as a Christian polemic against Judaism.

From examining the world behind the libretto of *Messiah*, it appears, for example, that the Hallelujah chorus rejoices not so much over the birth or resurrection of Jesus but, rather, explicitly over the "dashing in pieces" of unbelievers in Christ Jesus, including "the people [of Israel]," "the Jews."[3] This chorus apparently exults, in part, in the belief that God has rejected Judaism in favor of Christianity.

Today, perhaps not surprisingly, this anti-Judaic schadenfreude aspect of *Messiah* has been forgotten, and bringing it up, I've found, is by and large profoundly unwelcome. Intellectually, the notion that Handel's oratorio might contain anti-Judaic sentiments isn't particularly doubtful, but emotionally, for many, the idea will remain highly controversial.

So is it only in the interest of dispassionate historical accuracy that I delve into my topic? I recognize that all books involve advocacy of one sort or another. In calling attention to an anti-Judaic aspect in the world of Handel's *Messiah*, I'm ultimately interested in resisting Christian triumphalism—that is, the (widespread) bad habit of vaingloriously assuming that traditional Christian religious beliefs and practices are superior to all others and should prevail over them. My aims aren't anti-Christian. And they're not even anti-triumph as such. They're anti-triumphalist.

As a frequent public lecturer I have long come to recognize, even among seemingly level-headed people in the United States and elsewhere, a burgeoning, unexamined Christian triumphalism that is often linked to an, at best, unconscious, breezy contempt for Judaism.[4] Uncritical or overappreciative responses to Handel's *Messiah* can fuel such triumphalism, but—I hope against hope—historically better-informed critical responses might help to combat it.

My hope is also that this book will provide a useful model of how to handle pieces of music that are, or turn out to be, ethically troubling: not by evasion, not through bowdlerization, but by exploring the fullest and most thought-provoking contexts in which to comprehend and interpret the works.

I won't claim that Christian rejoicing against Jews *above others* is the problem with *Messiah*. It isn't. Instead, arguing from the viewpoints of both secular and biblical ethics, I'll take the problem with this oratorio to be that it rejoices against Jews *at all*.

And I certainly won't, and wouldn't, suggest eliminating *Messiah* from the concert repertory. Quite the contrary. What I am pushing for is a fuller understanding of the ethical and theological issues raised in this aesthetically magnificent work.

HOW THIS BOOK IS ORGANIZED

I end this chapter with a few words on how this book has been put together.

Chapter 2 is an essay that can be read on its own. It explores in detail only the aspects of Handel's *Messiah* that I think contribute most significantly to its theological anti-Judaism.

To write the essay, I pursued essentially only original research, and so you won't find me making references to the many previously published books on *Messiah*. You might reasonably wonder, If *Messiah* is indeed contemptuous toward Judaism, why don't those other books properly discuss the subject? Am I not casting a flood of light where heretofore there was no darkness?[5] I can't respond authoritatively, but I will say that those studies reflect other interests and focus on other aspects of Handel's multifaceted work.

Tassilo Erhardt has recently published a magnificent book, in German, on the full range of *Messiah*'s theological concerns, *Händels Messiah: Text, Musik, Theologie* (2007). In my opinion, this is the best book ever written on *Messiah*, and I hope a top-level English translation will be published soon. Erhardt calls great attention to Christian theological disagreement with Judaism in *Messiah*.

My independent inquiry, however, focuses not on anti-Judaism in the ethically acceptable sense of Christian disagreement with Judaism but on anti-Judaism in the ethically troubling sense of Christian *disdain* for Judaism. (The difference between disagreement and disdain isn't always clear, or properly recognized when it is clear, but wherever there is schadenfreude, the line has no doubt been crossed.)

Because previous modern-day books on *Messiah* don't directly engage my specific topic, I went—indeed, had to go—to original seventeenth- and eighteenth-century sources. In the rare-book rooms of the New York Public Library and elsewhere I made some remarkable discoveries about Jennens's libretto. Chief among them was that the various puzzling—not musically motivated—revisions in *Messiah* of wordings from the King James Bible and the *Book of Common Prayer* did not originate with Jennens. And the interpretive import of these revisions is crucial to understanding the anti-Judaic aspects already built in to the setup of Jennens's libretto.

For his textual revisions Jennens relied significantly, for example, on the learned critiques of the King James Bible in Henry Hammond's books *A Paraphrase and Annotations upon all the Books of the New Testament, Briefly Explaining all the Difficult Places Thereof* (1653) and *A Paraphrase and Annotations upon the Books of the Psalms, Briefly Explaining the Difficulties Thereof* (1659).[6]

These were not out-of-the-way reference works. Jennens's renowned contemporary, the great English author Samuel Johnson (1709–84), for example, considered Hammond's to be the best commentary on the New Testament, as James Boswell reported in his biography, *Life of Samuel Johnson* (1791). Hammond's research has a strong, if conventional, anti-Judaic bent. I'm not sure why previous research on the *Messiah* libretto missed his work.

Following, then, upon the main essay in chapter 2, I provide the complete eighteenth-century text of *Messiah*, fully identifying for the first time the historical sources of Jennens's various textual emendations. Chapter 3 also prints complete quotations of parallel passages from the Old or New Testament in the contemporaneous readings of the King James Bible. Further, it provides my own paraphrase and annotations briefly explaining all of the biblical passages in *Messiah*.

This part of the book can be read on its own as a short general commentary on the whole oratorio, albeit one that reinforces the findings of the main essay—and to save readers from having to flip back and forth, some earlier material is repeated here in the commentary.

All of this material—the essay in chapter 2 and the annotated libretto in chapter 3—is designed for both lay readers and scholars. I hope to have met the requirements of original, academic inquiry in history, music, and religion,[7] but I've tried to write in such a way that the discussion will be readily comprehensible to interested readers with little or no background in any of these areas. I've sought, then, to accommodate the needs and interests of the broadly diverse audiences made up of scholars and laypeople that I'm familiar with from lecturing on the topic at various academic, cultural, and religious institutions.

I should also mention that my frequent references to "traditional Christianity" and "traditional Judaism" are to be read neither as normative (that is to say, as using *traditional* to mean "orthodox" or "in the right") nor as derogatory. I employ the word *traditional* simply and nonpejoratively according to sense 1(a) from the Merriam-Webster dictionary's entry for *tradition*: "an inherited, established, or customary pattern of thought, action, or behavior." There are, of course, myriad forms of Christianity and Judaism. I focused on only some relevant central aspects of belief and practice that fall within their mainstream traditions.

Scriptural passages not taken from the King James Bible or *Book of Common Prayer* are my own translations.

The conventions of biblical citation can be confusing. "Genesis 1:1,3" (i.e., without a space after the comma) means verse 1 and

verse 3 from chapter 1 in the book of Genesis; "Matthew 1:1, 3"
(i.e., with a space after the comma) means verse 1 from chapter 1,
and all of chapter 3 in the book of Matthew.

Some readers will be puzzled by the apparently inconsistent use
of *Lord* and Lord in quotations from the Bible. The King James
Bible renders this word with uppercase letters at whichever places
the titles *Adon* or *Adonai* in the Hebrew source texts of its Old
Testament are, or appear to be, referring to God. The same ortho-
graphical convention is observed whenever God's name, the Tetragrammaton (i.e., "word of four letters"), or *YHWH*, appears in the
Hebrew source texts. Though in Judaism it is traditionally too holy
to be spoken, God's name is nowadays often fully rendered by Christians either as *Yahweh* or, erroneously, as *Jehovah*. Owing to this
sanctity of the name *YHWH*, the title *Adonai*—a plural-of-majesty,
derived from the singular *Adon*, "Lord" or "Sir"—has traditionally
been spoken in Hebrew worship at those places where the written
texts indicate *HWHY* (i.e., Hebrew is read from right to left). In
Hebrew texts the consonants *HWHY* appear "pointed" with the
vowels from the word *Adonai*, to help people reading aloud to remember to pronounce the latter when they textually encounter the
former. The original pronunciation of the Tetragrammaton, a special utterance that was spoken only by priests for certain situations
in the Temple liturgy (i.e., prior to the destruction of the Jerusalem
Temple in the year 70), is in fact now unknown.[8]

❖ ❖ ❖

Writing this book was not fun. There is a lot of material here that I
and my fellow Handel enthusiasts would prefer not to hear. But we
do need to hear it, don't we?

II

REJOICING AGAINST JUDAISM IN HANDEL'S *MESSIAH*

Across North America, performances of Handel's oratorio *Messiah*—many of them "sing-ins," with the audience joining in for the choruses—are musical highlights of the Christmas season. Christians, Jews, and others come together to delight in one of the consummate masterpieces of Western music.

The high point, inevitably, is the Hallelujah chorus, familiar not only from countless concerts and recordings but also from its use in less lofty surroundings, from Mel Brooks's *History of the World, Part I*, where it signifies the origins of music among cavemen, to recent television ads depicting frantic bears' ecstatic relief in chancing upon Charmin toilet paper in the woods.

So my fellow *Messiah* lovers may be surprised to learn that the work was meant not for the Christmas season but for Lent. What's more, they might be downright shocked to hear that the Hallelujah chorus was designed in a way that apparently rejoices, in significant part, over the destruction of Jerusalem and the Second Temple in the year 70 CE, a horrific event that until recently most Christians construed as divine retribution on Judaism for its failure to accept Jesus as God's promised messiah.

No doubt some *Messiah* lovers will want immediately to object to any notion of the oratorio's rejoicing even in part against

Judaism, on the grounds that, as an impresario, Handel would not have allowed himself to be thought of as biting the hand that fed him: biographers and enthusiasts have told us repeatedly that large numbers of Jews attended the original performances of Handel's Israelite oratorios, contributing significantly to the success of Handel's concerts.[1] They haven't, however, actually offered any good evidence for this remarkable claim.[2]

In truth, the vast majority of Jews in eighteenth-century London were simply too poor to attend such events, and the population of wealthy Jews in London was certainly nowhere near great enough to provide *large* numbers for Handel's performances. This can be readily demonstrated, for example, in the detailed historical research of Harold Pollins, in *Economic History of the Jews in England* (1982), and Todd M. Endelman, in *The Jews of Georgian England, 1714–1830* (1979).

Observant Jews would in any event have balked at the frequent public exclaiming of the sacred name of God in Handel's many Israelite oratorios, even though the word *Jehovah* was a Christian misunderstanding of the Tetragrammaton (*YHWH*), the name of God that, for Jews, is too holy to be spoken.

As for *Messiah*, Handel's first London performances, for example, closed on 29 March 1743 (in the Julian calendar), the equivalent of 15–16 Nissan 5503 in the Jewish calendar—that is to say, on Passover. Can we reasonably imagine *many* Jews of Handel's London attending his concerts during or right before one of the most widely observed Jewish holidays?

While we are on the topic, there is a related popular myth that needs to be dispelled at the outset. My fellow Handel admirers often assert that the composer's practice of writing oratorios on ancient Israelite subjects (for example, *Israel in Egypt* and *Judas Maccabaeus*) is "pro-[*modern-*]Jewish." What they don't realize is that although Handel and his contemporaries certainly did have a high opinion of the characters populating their Old Testament, this was only because Christians had already for many centuries thought of the righteous ancient Israelites as proto-Christian believers in God's expected messiah, Jesus of Nazareth, namely Jesus Christ. (That is to say, these righteous ancient Israelites were not thought of, as it were, as proto-Orthodox, Conservative, Reform, or Reconstructionist Jews.)

This is why, for example, at bars 38–45 and, most strikingly, at the closing eight bars of the chorus "And the children of Israel sighed" in his oratorio *Israel in Egypt*, Handel can set the words "And [the Hebrew people's] cry came up unto God" to the melody of the first phrase from the Lutheran hymn "Christ lag in Todesbanden," a musical quotation that makes perfect sense from a traditional Christian perspective but no sense from a modern Jewish perspective.

Traditional Christianity, then, often taught that in its time and place—namely, *before* the advent of Jesus—the Jewish religion was "good." The influential theologian William Warburton (1698–1779) echoed this view clearly and forcefully in his widely read *The Divine Legation of Moses Demonstrated* (1766): "Had the Mosaic Religion [that is to say, not modern but *ancient* Judaism] been *absolutely good*, that is, *good* for all men as well as for the Jews, it had certainly never been *abolished*. . . . It was *relatively good*, [we Christians should] say, as it fully answered the design of God who gave it; which was, to preserve a chosen People . . . and to prepare the way for the further Revelation of a Religion *absolutely good* [i.e., Christianity], or a Religion for the use of all Mankind" (his italics).

How, then, did the Christians in Handel's and his librettist Charles Jennens's milieu view Judaism and those Jews who lived among them (that is to say, at a time well *after* the advent of Jesus)?

Consider, as a first relevant source, the writings of the eminent Anglican preacher Robert South (1634–1716), who in "Jesus of Nazareth Proved the True and Only Promised Messiah," from his *Sermons Preached upon Several Occasions* (1737), states: "To reckon up all the pretences that the *Jews* allege for their not acknowledging of [Jesus] Christ, would be as endless as the tales and fooleries of their rabbis, a sort of men noted for nothing more than two very ill qualities, to wit, that they are still given to invent and write lies."

Consider also, moreover, that according to the likewise eminent preacher and theologian Isaac Barrow (1630–77), in his "Of the Imperfection of the Jewish Religion," from *The Works of the Learned Isaac Barrow . . . Sermons and Expositions upon All the Articles in The Apostles Creed* (1716): "Jews . . . have always (since [the days of old, something that is certainly] well known and observed in the world) been reputed . . . vain and superstitious . . . extremely proud and arrogant, churlish and sour, ill-natured and false-hearted toward all men; [they are] not good or kind, yea not so much as just or true toward any but themselves: . . . deservedly [they strike us Christians as] offensive and odious; . . . They have been long . . . the scorn and obloquy of all nations."

These sources were most probably familiar to the librettist of *Messiah* (who owned copies of both books, and hundreds of others like them). What South and Barrow say is also, I've found, altogether typical of prevalent mainstream sentiments in the Christianity of the eighteenth century. I looked long and hard to find evidence of contemporaneous Christian disagreement with such ways of thinking. I did find *some*, but the fact is that the historical sources that are directly or indirectly relevant to Handel's *Messiah* have virtually nothing positive or in any way loving-thy-neighbor to say on the subject of Jews and Judaism, and very little to say that is even neutral.

In my discussion of anti-Judaic aspects in *Messiah*, I draw on representative historical sources. Most of the books I cite are ones that were demonstrably known to the librettist of *Messiah*, and several of them were among the best-known and most widely consulted religious books in the seventeenth and eighteenth centuries. These historical sources of course discuss many other religious aspects as well, but so far as I could see, none that is incompatible with their theological anti-Judaism.

THE LIBRETTIST'S GENERAL APPROACH AND CONCERNS

The *Messiah* libretto was created by Charles Jennens (c. 1700–73). Jennens was a gentleman scholar of considerable erudition, and he was a friend of Handel's. For *Messiah*, he gave Handel a series of scriptural passages either quoted verbatim from the King James Version of the Bible and the Church of England's *Book of Common Prayer* or revised on the basis of religious and linguistic suggestions in the scholarly and popular biblical reference works he evidently consulted.

In England at this time the philosophy called Deism was taking hold among certain prominent thinkers and writers. Deism taught that God had simply created the cosmos and then let it run its course without divine intervention. Jennens must have been deeply troubled by the spread of Deism. Traditional Christianity, then as now, rested on the belief that God did indeed break into history, for example, by taking human form in Jesus. For Jennens and his sphere Deism represented a serious menace. If Deism were to catch on generally, it would mean the collapse of Christendom. No longer would Jesus have died for the world's sin. Deism would effectively make Christianity irrelevant.

Deists argued that Jesus was neither the divine Son of God nor the Messiah. Since Christian writers had habitually considered Jews the most grievous enemies of their religion, some came to suppose that Deists obtained anti-Christian ammunition from rabbinical scholars. For example, the Anglican bishop Richard Kidder, a popular preacher and writer, claimed in his huge treatise of 1684–99 on Jesus as the Messiah that "the Deists among us, who would run down our revealed religion, are but underworkmen to the Jews."

The title of Kidder's book says it all: *A Demonstration of the Messias, in Which the Truth of the Christian Religion Is Proved, against All the Enemies Thereof; but Especially against the Jews*. Jennens owned a 1726 edition, and he presumably consulted it attentively: Kidder's is a key work among the many contemporary publications on the nature and mission of Jesus as God's messiah, a book whose list of contents happens to read like a blueprint for Jennens's *Messiah* libretto.[3] Many of the biblical verses that Kidder discusses are used by Jennens. But much more significant than this is Jennens's apparent reliance on Kidder for some particular juxtapositions and formal placements of the Bible verses in *Messiah*.

At the time of *Messiah*'s composition and first performances, Kidder's book was still a well-appreciated work. For example, John Boswell, in his *A Method of Study; or, An Useful Library . . . Containing Some Directions for the Study of Divinity* (1738–43), a publication also found in Jennens's library, was in the 1740s recommending two of the books we know Jennens owned as the very best available studies proving that Jesus was God's promised messiah: Kidder's *Demonstration* and John Pearson's *Exposition of the Creed* (1710).[4]

Central to Kidder and his many like-minded readers, including Jennens, is a mode of interpretation called "typology," which here means that events in the Old Testament point ahead to events in

Christian history. This foreshadowing occurs not only through explicit prophecy and fulfillment but also through the more mysterious implied spiritual anticipation of Christian "antitypes" in Old Testament "types."

George Lavington, in his *The Nature and Use of a Type* (1724), provides a helpful contemporaneous explanation of biblical typology and the fundamental relationship between the Old and New Testaments: "The word *type* signifies in general a *figure, pattern*, or *example*: and in a theological sense may be defined *a sign or symbol of some more excellent future thing, originally designed by God to prefigure that future thing.* And what answers to the type, what is prefigured or foreshown by it, is called the *antitype*. . . . The former is the sign, the shadow, and the resemblance; the latter the thing signified, the substance, and the truth. . . . The *end and design* of all [biblical] *types* in general is to *prefigure Christ and his kingdom*. The Old Testament, and *Moses*, and the Law, and *Judaism* are *typical* of [their *antitypes*] the New Testament, and Jesus, and the Gospel, and Christianity" (his italics).

Employing the word *type* in this sense is, notably, itself biblical. In the New Testament at Romans 5:14, for example, the apostle Paul describes the first man Adam as a *type* (in transliterated Greek, *tupos* or *typos*) of "the one to come" (Jesus, the *antitype*).

Typological and prophetic thinking was a driving force behind Kidder's book and behind Jennens's choice and juxtaposition of biblical texts in his libretto. In *Messiah*, Old and New Testament selections stand fundamentally in such an alignment.[5]

But Jennens had the discernment to realize that books and pamphlets alone couldn't adequately combat the fruits of his enemies' labors. Jennens turned to the power of music, approaching the great George Frideric Handel with a new oratorio libretto. Handel, the best composer in England, was (like Johann Sebastian Bach) born in 1685 in Germany, but from the 1710s until his death in 1759, he was based in London. Handel had earlier collaborated with Jennens on the oratorio *Saul* and on the moral cantata *L'allegro, il penseroso ed il moderato*.

What better means for Jennens to comfort disquieted Christians against the faith-busting wiles of non-Christians than to draw on the force and emotions of art over and above the reasons and determinations of argument?

Messiah does exactly this, and at the Hallelujah chorus it can be heard to deliver a euphoric climax of Christian rejoicing, in substantial and specially problematic part, I suggest, against Judaism.

The issue of *Messiah*'s (central) anti-Deism is a topic amply covered in several excellent recent books on Handel. The facet of *Messiah*—and it is only one aspect of the oratorio—that I explore here is its (secondary) anti-Judaism. It's worth emphasizing that this aspect is a matter not of so-called racial antisemitism but of exulting over the misfortune and the believed everlasting divine condemnation of the religion of Judaism and its practitioners. Though not a matter of indifference, for present purposes I am agnostic on the prickly question of whether disdain for Judaism can or must lead to "racial" antisemitism. Rejoicing about the downfall of Judaism and its replacement by Christianity is surely an already sufficiently troubling and attention-worthy phenomenon.[6]

In this examination, precision of language is vital. I do appreciate that *anti-Judaism* and *anti-Jewish* are profoundly incendiary terms. Doubtless all forms of Christianity, to varying degrees, are "anti-Jewish" in the limited and untroubling sense that they do not concur with the various forms of Judaism that reject Jesus as God's promised messiah. I see no problem with religious *disagreement*. More difficult, and emotionally controversial, is the question of whether anti-Judaism in its general sense of "disagreeing with

Judaism" ever spills over into anti-Judaism in its more specific and, I should think, morally repugnant sense of "fostering contempt for Judaism."

Some will object that if one seeks contemptuous anti-Judaism in Jennens's and Handel's England, one will of course find it. Revealing *past* anti-Judaism is not my purpose, though. Drawing on previously unknown or underexplored historical sources, I seek, rather, to illuminate Handel's still-living masterpiece for today's listeners. My research interests here are "exegetical": to probe plausible meanings of this individual, ever-timely artwork.

Of course, that eighteenth-century Christian works would project sentiment of any kind against Judaism is altogether unremarkable. That Handel's beloved *Messiah*, "the world's favorite Christmas piece,"[7] should be said to do so, however, does come as a fiercely unwelcome surprise to many. A great number of my fellow *Messiah* lovers, I've found, believe that Handel's oratorio is a repository of only the true, the beautiful, the good, and the just. They hold *this* exceptional, great choral work to be utterly ageless, and to be soundly comforting and felicitous—not to any extent affected by its historical contexts, and assuredly not in any way unsavory or discomfiting. After two and a half centuries, *Messiah* remains deeply and unproblematically meaningful to hundreds of thousands, if not millions, of people around the world.

I would say, then, that schadenfreude toward Judaism is certainly not the whole story of *Messiah*, but again, I do contend that it is one significant, if today generally unrecognized, *aspect* of the narrative. And as we'll see, Handel's musical setting, too, even if to a much lesser extent than Jennens's libretto, apparently has its own contributions to make on the issue.

Jennens and Handel, as you'd expect, followed the social and religious spirit of their times, and I don't intend to condemn, excuse, or laud these great men for this. Instead, I hope to raise awareness about the many ideas, today insufficiently understood and often disquieting, that are reflected in Handel's still-living and ever-present work. A choral masterpiece much celebrated at present for bringing together people of diverse backgrounds was also apparently designed in a way that, in significant part, rejoices against Jews and Judaism.

THE CORE OF THE REJOICING AGAINST JUDAISM

Prophetic Psalm 2

Immediately preceding the Hallelujah chorus in *Messiah* are four movements whose texts come from Psalm 2. We are not at the libretto's sections concerning the birth or resurrection of Jesus, but at the narrative about his immediate disciples' preaching the gospel soon after the resurrected Jesus has ascended into heaven. This later section is the crux of our story, and we will look at it in some detail.

The scene leading to the Hallelujah chorus starts with the thunderous bass aria "Why do the nations so furiously rage together?" These are the opening words of Psalm 2, as revised by Jennens.

I'll mark the text here with underlining to show the differences in wording among Jennens's compiled libretto and his various sources. These sources include the *Book of Common Prayer* and the King James Bible, along with the important previously overlooked source I uncovered while doing research in the marvelous rare book room at Harvard University: Henry Hammond's imposing commentary, *A Paraphrase and Annotations upon the Books of the Psalms, Briefly Explaining the Difficulties Thereof* (1659):

Jennens's Messiah *Libretto*

Why do the nations so furiously rage together, and why do the people imagine a vain thing? The kings of the earth rise up, and the rulers take counsel together against the Lord and against his Anointed.

Book of Common Prayer, Psalm 2:1–2

Why do the <u>heathen</u> so furiously rage together: and why do the people imagine a vain thing? The kings of the earth <u>stand</u> up, and the rulers take counsel together: against the Lord, and against his Anointed.

King James Bible, Psalm 2:1–2

Why do the <u>heathen</u> rage, <u>and the</u> people imagine a vain thing? The kings of the earth <u>set themselves</u>, and the rulers take counsel together, against the LORD, and against his anointed, <u>saying</u> . . .

Hammond, Psalm 2:1–2

Why do the <u>heathen</u> (*margin*, "nations") rage (*margin*, "<u>conspire</u>, <u>assemble</u>"), <u>and the</u> people imagine a vain thing? The kings of the earth <u>set themselves</u> (*margin*, "rise up"), and the rulers take counsel (*margin*, "<u>assemble</u>") together against the LORD and against his anointed, <u>saying</u> . . .

What interpretive possibilities are opened up or reinforced with the libretto's adoption of key textual variants from Hammond?

Especially significant for *Messiah* is the change at Psalm 2:1 from *heathen* to *nations*. An advantage of the word *nations* is that it can be easily understood to include "the Jews" when the Psalm passage is prophetically applied to New Testament narratives, as Hammond indeed expressly notes in his commentary: "A *conspiration* and complotting of wicked men is most agreeable to the *mystical* and *prophetical* notion, that which is fulfilled in the *Jews* and *Ro-mans'* conjunction against *Christ*, those being the *goyim nations* (so the word literally must be rendered [that is to say, not as "hea-then"] . . .) and in the same sense *lehummim populi*, in the latter part of this verse (as *nations* and *people* are all one) which *con-spired* to put him to *death*" (his italics).

No one would have understood the King James Bible and *Book of Common Prayer*'s word *heathen* at Psalm 2:1 to refer to Jews or Judaism. In eighteenth-century England even children would know that a Jew is not a heathen, for example, from the famous hymn writer Isaac Watts's wildly popular and constantly reprinted *Divine Songs Attempted in Easy Language for the Use of Children* (1715; given here according to the 1735 edition), which includes the stanza (his italics):

> LORD, I ascribe it to thy Grace,
> And not to Chance, as others do,
> That I was born of *Christian* Race,
> And not a *Heathen* or a *Jew*.

Several nonmusicians have suggested to me that Jennens may simply have thought the word *nations* would be easier to sing than the word *heathen*. I very much doubt this was the case. For one thing, the word *nations* is not easier to sing. For another, Jennens *did* have Handel set the word *heathen* elsewhere in *Messiah* where the word *nations* could have been appropriate to the sense of the text, namely at "Rejoice greatly, O Daughter of Sion," movement no. 18:

> Rejoice greatly, O Daughter of *Sion*, shout, O Daughter of *Jerusa-lem*; behold thy King cometh unto thee:
> He is the righteous Saviour, and He shall speak Peace unto the Heathen.

We see the same situation, for example, at "Tell It Out among the Heathen," movement no. 62 in Jennens and Handel's later oratorio *Belshazzar*:

Tell it out among the heathen,
That the Lord is King.

We know, further, that Jennens's set of revisions to biblical texts for *Messiah* can't simply be explained as musically motivated, for example, from the fact that the epigraph for his libretto—that is, words which were not meant to be set to music—takes up a whole series of alterations to the King James text of 1 Timothy 3:16 that were recommended, I've discovered, in Hammond's *A Paraphrase and Annotations upon all the Books of the New Testament* (1653):

Jennens's Messiah *Epigraph*
And without Controversy, great is the Mystery of Godliness: God was manifested in the Flesh, justified by the Spirit, seen of Angels, preached among the *Gentiles*, believed on in the World, received up in Glory.

King James Bible, 1 Timothy 3:16
And without controversy, great is the mystery of godliness: God was <u>manifest</u> in the flesh, justified <u>in</u> the Spirit, seen of angels, preached <u>unto</u> the Gentiles, believed on in the world, received up <u>into</u> glory.

Hammond, 1 Timothy 3:16
And without controversy great is the mystery of godliness, God was <u>manifest</u> in (*margin*, "manifested <u>by</u>") the flesh, justified <u>in</u> (*margin*, "by") the spirit, seen of Angels, preached <u>unto</u> (*margin*, "among") the Gentiles, believed on in the world, received up <u>into</u> (*margin*, "in" or "<u>with</u>") glory.

Presumably, then, if Jennens adopted Hammond's changes to 1 Timothy 3:16 for textual reasons, his changes taken from Hammond for Psalm 2 may well have been similarly motivated.

The early, historical sense of the Hebrew text of Psalm 2:1 would be something like the following:

> *Why do the gentiles so furiously rage together, and why do these foreign peoples contemplate an idle thing: the notion of prevailing against God's anointed one, King David of Israel?*

For contemporaneous Christian understandings, the historical reading is the "sign," the "shadow," or the "resemblance." The "thing signified," the "substance," or the "truth," however, would be, in Hammond's and Jennens's traditional Christian interpretation, this typological or prophetic reading:

> *Why do the nations—the Romans and Jews—so furiously rage together against Jesus, and why do the people* of Israel[8]—*"the Jews"— contemplate an idle thing: the notion of prevailing against the Lord God and against God's "Anointed One" (that is,* the Messiah*), Christ Jesus (and thus against his message)?*

The idea in the earlier, pre-Christian understandings of Psalm 2 is that here neither the *goyim* nor the *lehummim* are Israelites; that is to say, both of these particular groups who torment God's "anointed one," customarily understood to be King David of Israel, are decidedly *non*-"Jews." The question is, to whom will *goyim* refer in Christian prophetic or typological readings of the first phrase of the psalm?

I expect that some readers will immediately object that no matter how Jennens rendered the word *goyim* into English, he can't ever have imagined *Jews* to be meant prophetically here at Handel's bass aria, even with the possibly more comprehensive word *nations*, because Jennens must have known that the Psalm's Hebrew source word *goyim* always means non-Jews.

But this understanding of the word *goyim* as solely "non-Jews" is true only in postbiblical parlance. Jennens, an accomplished student of the Bible, most probably knew that in the Hebrew texts of the Old Testament the Israelites, too, are in fact at times referred to with the words *goy* and *goyim*.[9] So, biblically, the words *goyim* and *nations* can include gentiles and Jews.

Here one might object that Jennens substituted *nations* for Psalm 2 in Handel's aria simply because he thought it was a better or more accurate translation for *goyim* than *heathen*, and not because of anything concerning Jews or gentiles. But if that were so, presumably Jennens would likewise have changed the King James Bible's *heathen* to *nations* for Handel's earlier-mentioned aria, "Rejoice greatly, O Daughter of Sion." This aria's middle section closes with the text of Jennens's rendering of Zechariah 9:10: "He is the righteous Saviour, and He shall speak Peace unto the Heathen [the Hebrew source word here is *goyim*]." Jennens is apparently content, in *Messiah*, to have Zechariah 9:10 point to God's messiah's clearly speaking words of peace to only the *gentiles*.[10]

Now those with close knowledge of the King James version of the New Testament will recall that Psalm 2:1 is quoted in Acts 4:25–27 and that the King James translators straightforwardly understand the ones who "imagine vain things" to be "the people *of Israel*." Acts 4 there reads: "[God] by the mouth of thy servant David hast said [at Psalm 2:1], 'Why did the heathen rage, and *the people* imagine vain things? The kings of the earth stood up, and the rulers were gathered together against the Lord, and against his Christ.' For of a truth against thy holy child Jesus, whom thou hast anointed, both Herod and Pontius Pilate, with the Gentiles, and the people *of Israel* were gathered together [against Jesus, at his crucifixion]."

Hammond and Jennens allowed for a certain heightening, then, of the blame placed on so-called Old Israel in Acts 4:25–27 ("the people *of Israel*," namely "the Jews"), by changing the first phrase of Psalm 2's *heathen* (which predicts only the Romans raging against Jesus at his crucifixion) to *nations* (which predicts the Romans and Jews—something neither the English rendering *heathen* nor *gentiles* would have done, seeing that in biblical Hebrew, Jews may be among the *goyim*, but in English, a Jew is neither a *heathen* nor a *gentile*).[11] Thus, if in the King James texts from Psalm 2 and Acts 4 "the Jews" simply *imagine* a vain thing against Jesus, in *Messiah*, then, "the Jews" will also *furiously rage* in violence against Jesus.

The rest of the text from this aria, if it in fact describes the forces against Jesus as universal or at least as predominantly gentile (Psalm 2:2, "The kings *of the earth* rise up, and the rulers take counsel together, against the Lord and against his Anointed"), would cast doubt on the idea that Hammond and Jennens are intensifying, however slightly, any anti-Judaic sentiment with their revision of Psalm 2.

But on the contrary, Christians have traditionally understood Psalm 2:2 typologically in light of the Gospel of Luke's passion narrative and its Jews, as dictated by the glossing of Psalm 2 at Acts 4:25–27 (the passage quoted earlier). The "kings" are understood not generally but are specifically taken to point to the New Testament's Herod Antipas, the tetrarch of Galilee (Herod Antipas has traditionally been understood as Jewish; and he was a son of Herod the Great, who was called "King of the Jews"), along specifically with Pilate the Roman governor of Judea (representative of the "king," Caesar). The "rulers," further, are traditionally understood to refer specifically to the members of the Jewish Sanhedrin, and the "Lord's Anointed" to God's messiah, Jesus.

Thus, for example, Hammond, in his *Paraphrase and Annotations upon the Psalms*, writes of Psalm 2:2, "*Herod*, and *Pilate*, and the Jewish Sanhedrin make a solemn opposition . . . against Jesus . . . *Acts*.iv.27"; and Samuel Humphreys writes similarly of Psalm 2:2, in his *The Sacred Books of the Old and New Testament, Recited at Large and Illustrated with Critical and Explanatory Annotations, Carefully Compiled from the Commentaries and Other Writings of . . . Eminent Authors, Ancient and Modern* (1735–39), "Herod and Pontius Pilate, and the rulers of Israel (Acts iv.27.) will conspire against Christ [Jesus]."

In summary, where for Psalm 2's earliest (BCE) readers the opening phrases will, in their context, have spoken clearly and forcefully first of *non*-Jews and then likewise of *non*-Jews, the oratorio *Messiah*, as is meant to be understood in typological light of the New Testament's use of Psalm 2:1 at Acts 4:27, can speak in the first instance of *included* Jews ("why do *the nations*") and in the next of *only* Jews ("why do *the people* [of Israel]").

And so at this portion of *Messiah*, where Jesus' disciples go out into the world to spread the gospel, just like in the corresponding narrative of Acts 1–4, the libretto is designed, it appears, in a way that, among other things, prophetically reminds listeners of Jewish Jerusalem's initial, crucifixion-provoking hostility toward Jesus. The libretto is further designed in a way that then rejoices at, among other things, the ensuing destruction of the city and its Temple (as taken to have been predicted by the preceding aria's text from Psalm 2, "Thou shalt break them with a rod of iron; thou shalt dash them in pieces like a potter's vessel"). That is to say, the Hallelujah chorus apparently exults, in significant part, over what would be taken as the essential deathblow to Judaism, with Christianity understood as sole legitimate heir of God's promises to ancient Israel.

Regarding "People" and "the Sons of Levi"

Jennens's use at various places in *Messiah* of the word *people* in and of itself shouldn't be understood to have a special meaning of "Israel," namely as "the Jews." If that were so, the text of the oratorio might be construed as singling out (ancient and modern) Jews for special reassurance at the very outset: "Comfort ye *my people* . . . speak ye comfortably to Jerusalem, and say unto her, that her iniquity is pardoned" (Isaiah 40:1–3), a situation that is hardly akin to Christian rejoicing in significant part over the downfall of Judaism as presaged by the destruction of the Temple.

On the contrary, the expression "*my* people" (that is, *God's* people) here in a Christian reading like Jennens's does not for a moment extend the comforting words of Isaiah to *modern* practitioners of Judaism who do not turn to belief in Jesus. In the world of *Messiah*, "my people" means Christian believers, and not post-Jesus Jews who don't accept Jesus. *Jerusalem*, here, in turn, refers not to Judaism but Christianity, as governed by New Testament understandings like that of Galatians 4:22–26, which reads: "It is written [at Genesis 16 and 21], that Abraham had two sons, the one by a bondmaid [i.e., the slave Hagar, mother of Ishmael], the other by a freewoman [i.e., Sarah, the mother of Isaac]. . . . Which things are an allegory: for these are the two covenants [*KJV marginal note:* "*Or,* testaments"]; the one from the mount Sinai [i.e., where the Law of Moses was given—signifying *Old Israel*, Judaism], which gendereth to bondage, . . . But Jerusalem which is above is free [i.e., not the earthly "*Jerusalem which now is*," but the heavenly "*Jerusalem which is above*"—signifying *New Israel*, or Christianity]."

Whatever is to be made of the expression "the people" in Psalm 2 and Acts 4, some will object that *Messiah* simply can't be anti-

Judaic because the word *Jews* or *Judaism* is nowhere mentioned explicitly in Jennens's libretto.

In their view, the closest that the entire oratorio text comes to fully explicit mention of Jews is "the Sons of Levi," who are going to be "purified" such that they will "offer unto the Lord an offering in righteousness" (at no. 7 in the libretto). So, according to this argument, Jennens just might be making a *positive* statement about Jews!

But that is decidedly not how the passage, Malachi 3:3, was ever understood in the various sources from Jennens's library, and indeed I have never come across any remotely pro-Judaic readings from other traditional Christian authors elsewhere (that is to say, I've seen no readings in which Malachi is understood to mean that God will purify and preserve the Temple as a place where the worship will remain Jewish without eventually, or ever, becoming Christian).[12] What Malachi 3:3–4 basically says in traditional Christian readings is that the sons of Levi will be purified by leaving their Judaism behind altogether and becoming members of the "body of Christ," or the Christian Church.

Some of what Edward Wells, in his *An Help for the More Easy and Clear Understanding of the Holy Scriptures: Being the Twelve Lesser Prophets* (1723)—a book whose back-matter list of subscribers includes "Charles Jennens Esq; of Gopsal"—says of this passage is directed toward the destruction of Jerusalem and its Temple as a divine, purifying act: "[That is], after his [Jesus'] coming and the Jews' not receiving him as their Messiah, . . . he shall cause great afflictions to fall on the Jewish nation by the Romans [in the years 66–73 CE], which shall be so great as they may be compared to a fierce fire, whereby refiners separate the dross from the true gold and silver. . . . [Those Jews who accept Jesus and become Christians] shall be preserved at least finally or to eternal life; and even all of them [the believers in Jesus] shall be preserved from that common destruction, which shall befall the unbelieving Jews for their said unbelief of Christ, by the Romans' taking and destroying Jerusalem and the Temple."

Edward Pococke, in his *Commentaries on Hosea, Joel, Micah, and Malachi* (1740), likewise owned by Jennens, also takes Malachi 3:3 to mean that the "*purified* sons of Levi" are not practitioners of Judaism. Rather, they are those spiritual heirs of ancient Israel who follow Jesus (that is, *Christians*), whether as members of the clergy or as members of the laity.

Similarly, concerning Malachi 3:3, William Nicholls, in his *Commentary on the Book of Common-Prayer* (1712), which Jennens also owned, writes: "[The Lord] shall rectify the abuses in Ecclesiastical Affairs . . . [which] the Jewish Clergy, by their corrupt Traditions, shall have introduced. . . . [God] shall institute a [*Christian*] Ministry . . . which shall be more righteous."

In *Messiah*, the first three verses of Malachi 3 are set next to the text of Haggai 2:6–7, the latter rendered by Jennens as follows: "Thus saith the Lord of Hosts: Yet once a little while, and I will shake the Heavens and the Earth, the Sea, and the dry Land: And I will shake all Nations, and the *Desire of all Nations* [i.e., my messiah] shall come."

Significantly, Kidder's *Demonstration* on several occasions discusses Haggai 2 together with Malachi 3, and Kidder took Haggai 2:6–7 to point, in part, to God's destruction of "Jewish polity": "GOD hath given us notice, that he would put an end to the institutions of *Moses*, in the days of the MESSIAS. . . . The shaking of the heaven and earth signifies the destruction of the *Jewish* polity. . . . [T]he laws about sacrifice fell with the temple; and many fell with the city of *Jerusalem*; and when the *Jews* ceased to be a polity, their political laws were rendered null." That is to say, by way of paraphrase:

The Lord God has let us Christians know that God would put an end to Judaism at the dawning of the messianic age of Christianity, when God destroys the Temple and establishes the Christian Church.

Significantly, Haggai 2 and Malachi 3 are likewise linked in a number of other theological sources listed in Jennens's library.[13]

Worth noting, too, is the fact that traditional Christian understandings of Malachi 3:3 would be governed by what is said of "the sons of Levi"—the Jewish priesthood—in the New Testament at Hebrews 7:5,11–12, which reads: "[Regarding] *the sons of Levi*[:] . . . If therefore perfection were [to be found] by the Levitical priesthood (for under it *the people* [of Israel] received the law), what further need was there that another priest should rise after the order of Melchisedec, and not be called after the order of Aaron? For the priesthood being changed, there is made of necessity a change also of the law."

To readers unfamiliar with the King James Bible, several of this passage's expressions may require explanation. "The people," here, means Old Israel, "the Jews." "The law" is the Law of Moses. "Another priest" means God's messiah, Jesus. Melchisedec is the ancient king of Jerusalem and priest of the most high God—who prefigures God's messiah, Jesus, as king and priest (see Genesis 14:18–20,[14] Psalm 110:4, Hebrews 5:6,10). Aaron is the brother of Moses, and he, Aaron, is the ancestor of the Levitical priesthood (Exodus 28:1, 40:15, Numbers 25:13). "The priesthood being changed" refers to the purifying change from the priestly order of Aaron to the order of Melchisedec—that is to say, the move from the Temple to the church, namely from Judaism to Christianity (see Hebrews 6:20–7:22).

And so, to make the import of Hebrews 7:11–12 altogether clear, a paraphrase might read:

If the priesthood of Levi, tied to the Law of Moses and thus to "the Jews," could have achieved the perfection God intended, why did

God need to set up a different priesthood—namely the order of
Melchizedek, God's ancient king and priest who prefigures God's
messiah, Jesus—to take the place of the Levitical order of Aaron, the
brother of Moses? For if the old priesthood was changed, then the
old, "impure" way of the Law (Moses and "the Jews") must go with
it, so as to give place to the new, "pure" way of the Spirit (Jesus and
his followers).

In short: If complete qualification to stand before God could be found in Judaism and the Temple, why did God need to establish Christianity and the Christian Church?

Jennens may have additionally encountered these anti-Levite sentiments of Hebrews 6–7 when, in the 1710s, he was a student at Oxford's Balliol College and a member of the Oxford Music Club. Antony Alsop, likewise an Oxford student, had earlier written a libretto called *Messiah: A Christmas Song* (whose musical authorship is uncertain), in which, at the aria "Vouchsafe t' accept, O great High Priest," the Levitical and Christian priesthoods are contrasted as follows:

Aaron's priesthood must cease to be,
but *thine*'s to all eternity.

Furthermore, in Handel's oratorio *Athalia*, there is a "Chorus of young Virgins of the Tribe of *Levi*" with a "Chorus of *Israelitish* Priests and Levites" (that is, proto–Protestant Christians) who sing:

May God, from whom all Mercies spring,
Bless *the true Church*, and save the King.

Back to Psalm 2

Someone who knows the Anglican liturgy might object that the reason Psalm 2 appears right before the Hallelujah chorus is not that it can be read, in significant part, as a condemnation of Jews and Judaism, but rather, Psalm 2 would more likely have ended up there because it was one of the Psalms traditionally included in the Easter services of the Church of England.

Reference to the liturgy can indeed help explain why a bit of material from Psalm 2 appears earlier in *Messiah*, that is, close to the actual Easter portion of the oratorio's narrative. At the recitative no. 34, the libretto quotes Psalm 2:7 via its use in the New Testament at Hebrews 1:5, rendered by Jennens as: "Unto which of the Angels said He [God] at any time [as God does say of Jesus], *thou art my Son, this day have I begotten thee*?" (the italics indicate the verbatim quotation of Psalm 2:7b within Hebrews 1:5).

Among our sources from Jennens's library, Kidder, for example, explains that Psalm 2:7 is to be understood typologically of Jesus' resurrection, when Jesus is born anew from the metaphorical womb of his "mother," the earth, or the grave. The biblical basis for this is that at Jesus' resurrection, according to Acts 13:33, God declares Jesus to be God's Son. And so Jennens appropriately quotes biblical material corresponding with Psalm 2:7 at movement no. 34, near the Easter section of *Messiah*. (God's declaration of Sonship takes place with Jesus' *baptism*, however, in the Gospels; see Matthew 3:17, Mark 1:11, and Luke 3:22.)

So it was fitting for Jennens near his Easter portion of *Messiah* to use the part of Psalm 2 that was traditionally associated with Jesus' resurrection, namely verse 7, the passage that will have given rise to the reading of the Psalm in the Easter liturgy.

Other passages from Psalm 2 appear later in *Messiah*, however, right before the Hallelujah chorus, now evidently not because of the Easter liturgy but because these particular passages from Psalm 2 are drawn on significantly in Acts 4, the story of the disciples' preaching (soon after Jesus' ascension into heaven) to, among others, hostile Jews who are blamed for Jesus' crucifixion (at Acts 4:5–10). The run of Acts 4 corresponds precisely to Jennens's narrative content at this likewise post-resurrection-and-ascension portion of *Messiah*. Just like Acts 4, this section of *Messiah* is about not Easter but the disciples' later going out into the world to spread the gospel.[15]

Handel sets the text of Psalm 2:1–2 as a ferocious aria drawing on the tradition of what is called the *stile concitato*: he writes continually with repeated sixteenth notes, an Italian baroque convention for "militant" affects.[16] In Handel's setting, "the nations" and "the people of Israel" (i.e., "the Jews") are certainly rising up against the gospel of Jesus, in the warlike sense that Hammond emphasizes in his commentary on the Psalms.

At the end of scene 7 is a setting of Psalm 2:9, and now, for nearly the only time in *Messiah*, Jennens uses the King James Bible entirely as his Psalms source text rather than the *Book of Common Prayer*. Psalm 2:9 reads as follows in our sources:

> *Jennens's* Messiah *Libretto*
> Thou shalt break them with a rod of iron; thou shalt dash them in pieces like a potter's vessel.

> *Book of Common Prayer*, Psalm 2:9
> Thou shalt <u>bruise</u> them with a rod of iron: <u>and break</u> them in pieces like a potter's vessel.

> *King James Bible*, Psalm 2:9
> Thou shalt break them with a rod of iron; thou shalt dash them in pieces like a potter's vessel.

Because *Messiah* doesn't (need to) include verses 5–8, the word *them* of Psalm 2:9, in the tenor aria, can take as its extended antecedent "the nations" and also more specifically "the people [of

Israel]" ("the Jews"), or "the rulers [of the Jewish people]" (the Sanhedrin), from Jennens's version of Psalm 2:1–2 in the earlier bass aria.

In *Messiah* Jennens didn't have to contend with the traditional English translation's initial antecedent for the word *them* at verse 9, namely the "heathen" of verse 8a, there depicted as a grouping that will be inherited by the Anointed One. The King James Bible at Psalm 2:8 reads: "Ask of me [the Lord], and I shall give thee the heathen for thine inheritance, and the uttermost parts of the earth for thy possession."

This rendering of the first phrase from Psalm 2:8 would refer to the circumstance that the anointed one (traditionally, King David of Israel), in the context of the type, inherits dominion over "the heathen," namely the gentiles (non-Jews). The Anointed One, Christ Jesus, however, in the context of the antitype, inherits dominion over "the heathen," in this case namely the pagan unbelievers (non-Christian gentiles).

Had Jennens needed to contend with verse 8, he would presumably have followed Hammond's consistent suggestions for both verses 1 and 8 of Psalm 2, rendering *goyim* in both instances not as *heathen* but as *nations*.

In noting that *heathen* not only at Psalm 2:1 but also at 2:8 ought also to be rendered as *nations*, Hammond, in *A Paraphrase and Annotations upon the Books of the Psalms*, writes: "To this [Psalm 2:8 as type] is consequent, as a free and special mercy of God's, the enlarging of this his kingdom, not only to the inhabitants of Judea [i.e., "the Jews"], but to many other heathen nations . . . who were all subdued by *David*, through the power of God . . . and subjected to him. And so [as antitype, then,] upon the Resurrection and Ascension of Christ, by the wonderful blessing of God upon the preaching of the Apostles, not only the Jews (many thousands of them, Rev[elation] 7) but the heathens over all the world were brought in, to the faith of Christ [Jesus]."

Thus Hammond's suggested emendation at Psalm 2:8a would mean that the anointed one, King David, as type, inherits political dominion over "the nations," in his context namely the gentiles (seeing that David already had dominion over Israel). The Anointed One, Christ Jesus, however, as antitype, inherits dominion over "the nations," in his context namely Jews and gentiles.

If the antecedent "the heathen" must—by the rules of what is called lexical semantics—exclude "the Jews," the antecedent "the nations" can include them.

Even with "the heathen" at verse 8a, though, the whole verse may well be speaking also of Jews anyway: to "give the uttermost parts of the [flat] earth for [the Anointed One's] possession" probably includes all peoples, that is, gentiles and (Diaspora) Jews. The options depend on whether you read the word *and* at verse 8b as bringing either essentially a reiteration of 8a ("the outermost parts of the earth" as synonym for "the heathen") or an addition to 8a (the gentiles and Jews in verse 8b, as opposed to simply the heathen in 8a).

So who is this *thou* in Jennens's aria text "Thou shalt break them" if typologically his *them* is partly made up of Jews against Jesus?

In standard earlier English sources, Psalm 2:9 (this being the type) was conventionally understood in part to prefigure the destruction of Jerusalem in the years 66–73 CE (this being Psalm 2:9's first-century antitype). Jesus was thus the *thou* who destroys *them*, which includes specifically, though not exclusively, "the Jews." Hammond, for example, writes of verse 9: "[The typological reading is:] so shall Christ deal with his enemies, Jews and heathens, subdue some, and destroy the impregnable, and obdurate."

Hammond concludes, at his comments on the last verse of the Psalm, by condemning all unbelievers in Jesus, and in doing so he calls attention to God's *exemplary* rebuke of practitioners of Judaism: "[Those who] shall stand out, and not acknowledge his divine power, now [that] he [Jesus] is risen from the dead, but continue to provoke him still, they will certainly have their portion [eternally, in hell] with his enemies, be destroyed with the Jews, or after the like manner, that the Jews were, when the Romans came in, and wrought a horrid desolation among them, and only the believing Christian Jews, by obeying Christ's directions, were delivered out of it." (What Hammond is referring to at the end of this quotation is the traditional Christian belief that the risen Jesus rescued his Jerusalem followers by inspiring them to flee to the city of Pella before the Jewish war with Rome broke out in the years 66–73 CE.)

God's violent antipathy specifically first, though not exclusively, toward Jews is further reflected in the extremely well-known contemporary biblical commentary by Matthew Henry (a resource continually reprinted and still widely used devotionally by certain Christians today), *An Exposition of all the Books of the Old and New Testament: . . . with Practical Remarks and Observations* (1721–25), which, like *Messiah*, juxtaposes Psalm 2 and Revelation 11: "'Tis here [at Psalm 2:7–9] promised [to the Son], (1.) That his government shall be *universal*, he shall have *the heathen for his inheritance*; not the *Jews* only . . . GOD the Father *gives them* [baptized Christians] *to him* [Jesus] when by his Spirit and grace he works upon them to submit their necks to the yoke of the Lord JESUS. This is in part fulfilled; a great part of the gentile world received the Gospel when it was first preached, and CHRIST's throne was set up there where Satan's seat had long been: But it is to be yet further accomplished, when *the kingdoms of this world shall become the kingdoms of the Lord and of his Christ*, Rev[elation] xi. 15. *Who*

shall live when God doth this! (2.) That it [Christ's government]
shall be victorious, *Thou shalt break them, i.e.,* those of them that
oppose thy kingdom, *with a rod of iron,* v. 9. This was in part fulfilled when the nation of the *Jews,* those that persisted in unbelief
and enmity to CHRIST's Gospel, were destroyed [in 70 CE] by the
Roman power, which was represented, *Dan*[*iel*] ii. 40, by *feet of
iron,* as here by *a rod of iron.* It had a further accomplishment in the
destruction of the *pagan* Powers, when the Christian religion came
to be established [in the fourth century CE, under emperor Con-
stantine]; but it will not be completely fulfilled till all opposing rule,
principality and power, shall be finally put down, 1 *Cor*[*inthians*]
xv. 24. See *Psal*[*m*]. cx. 5, 6" (Henry's italics).

Consider likewise the commentary on Psalm 2 by Thomas
Fenton, in *Annotations on the Book of Job, and the Psalms; Collected from several Commentators, and Methodized and Improved*
(1732), who writes: "—*Dash them in pieces* &c.: The Word in the
Original signifies, not only to *break,* but also to *disperse.* Both these
Significations of it are implied in this Place, under the Notion of an
earthen Vessel, which, as being useless, is designedly broken, and
the pieces of it scatter'd abroad. And thus were the *Jewish* People dealt with; the Vengeance of Heaven, or of the *Messiah* from
Heaven, did as it were *dash them in pieces,* when *Jerusalem* was
destroyed by the Means of the *Romans*; and from that Time cast
them away, and dispers'd them throughout the World. Thus the Destruction and Desolation of the *Jews* for their Sins, are in like manner represented under the Idea of breaking a *Potter's Vessel,* and
throwing the Pieces away, as being unfit for Use, *Isa*[*iah*].xxx.14
and *Jer*[*emiah*].xix.11."

This understanding of Psalm 2's "*Thou* shalt break *them* with a
rod of iron [and] dash *them* in pieces" as a foretelling, in part, of

the destruction of Jerusalem had a long history (and in fact one still hears it preached today in certain churches).[17]

Concerning Psalm 2:8–9, the anonymous *A Paraphrase and Exposition of the Book of Psalms; Designed Principally for the Use of the Unlearned Reader* (1768) reports: "*Theodoret* [Bishop of Cyrrhus, fifth-century CE] doth well observe, that this is plainly a prophecy of the call of the gentiles to Christianity. . . . He observes too, that [Psalm 2:9] doth plainly allude to the final destruction of *Jerusalem*. And I must add, that so may the following words, 'thou shalt break them in pieces,' &c. to the dispersion of the *Jews*, which at this day is manifest to all."

The renowned author John Newton, in his *Messiah: Fifty Expository Discourses, on the Series of Scriptural Passages, which Form the Subject of the Celebrated Oratorio of Handel—Preached in the Years 1784 and 1785, in the Parish Church of St. Mary Woolnoth* (1786), also explains the text of Psalm 2, and indeed the whole of Jennens's libretto, with very much the same sort of traditional, and anti-Judaic, readings continually encountered in the books from Jennens's library and elsewhere, books published long before (and long after) the creating of *Messiah*. Newton himself appears to have been essentially ignorant of Handel's musical setting, but he provides useful evidence of how traditional preaching about a decade after Jennens's death still expected the Bible to be understood. On Psalm 2:9 Newton writes: "The Romans were the iron rod in his [the Lord's] hand, wherewith he dashed the Jewish nation to pieces [in the years 66–73]. Their fragments are scattered far and wide to this day, and who can gather them up? The Roman empire was likewise dashed to pieces in its turn. . . . I have been informed that the music to which this passage is set [in *Messiah*], is so well adapted to the idea that it expresses, as, in a manner, to startle those who hear it."

Newton writes further about Psalm 2 and its condemnation, specifically first, and *emblematically*, of "the Jews": "Opposition to MESSIAH and his kingdom, is . . . ruinous to those who engage in it. What did the Jews build, when they rejected the foundation stone which God had laid in Zion [Jesus, the antitype of Psalm 118:22]? They acted, as they thought, with precaution and foresight. They said, *If we let him thus alone, all men will believe on him; and the Romans shall come and take away both our place and our nation*, John xi.48. Foolish politicians! Did they preserve their city by crucifying the Son of God! The very evil they feared came upon them. Or rather, being abandoned of God to their own counsels, they brought it upon themselves. In a few years, the Romans, with whom they appeared so desirous to keep upon good terms, destroyed their city with an unheard of destruction, and exterminated them from the land. This was an emblem of the inevitable, total, irreparable ruin, which awaits all those who persist in rejecting the rule of MESSIAH. The nation, the individual, that will not serve him must surely perish."

Eighteenth-century Christian authors on religion continually make clear that the destruction of the Jerusalem Temple was God's abiding punishment of Israel (that is, not a temporary one like God's various earlier biblically depicted chastisements of Israel). Consider the example of Samuel Davies, president of the College of New Jersey (which later became Princeton University), who wrote in his *Sermons on the most useful and important Subjects, adapted to the Family and Closet* (1766), a book whose subscribers include "*Charles Jennens, Esq*;": "But, says he [the author of 1 Peter], 'if any man suffer as a *Christian* let him not be ashamed' [1 Peter, chapter 4,] *ver*[*se*] 16, for the time is come that judgment must begin at the house of GOD. He seems to have a particular view to the cruel persecution that a little after this was raised against the

Christians by the tyrant *Nero* [the Roman emperor, in 64 CE], and more directly to that which was raised against them everywhere by the seditious Jews, who were the most inveterate enemies of Christianity. The dreadful destruction of *Jerusalem* [in 66–73 CE] . . . was now at hand. And from the sufferings which Christians, the favourites of Heaven endured [in 64 CE], he infers how much more dreadful the vengeance would be which should fall upon their enemies the infidel Jews [in 66–73 CE]. . . . '*Them that obey not the gospel of GOD* [1 Peter 4:17]' is a description of the unbelieving Jews, to whom it was peculiarly applicable, and the apostle may have a primary reference to the dreadful destruction of their city and nation. . . . But I see no reason for confining the apostle's view entirely to this *temporal* destruction of the Jews: he seems to refer farther to that still more terrible destruction that awaits all that obey not the gospel in the *eternal* world [of heaven and hell]. . . . [W]hat shall become of rebels [like "the Jews"] in the world to come, the proper state of retribution?"

Newton's *Discourses*, having apparently taken for granted that Psalm 2:9 points, in part, to the destruction of the Jewish nation in 70 CE, then goes on to say: "[Jennens and Handel's tenor aria 'Thou shalt break them,' Psalm 2:9] prepares for the [Hallelujah chorus that follows at the] close of the second part of the Oratorio. [Christ's] enemies shall perish, his kingdom shall be established and consummated. And then all holy intelligent beings shall join in a song of triumph, *Hallelujah, for the Lord God Omnipotent reigneth*." (Thus Jews who don't believe in Jesus are, it appears, judged neither holy nor "intelligent.")[18]

Newton is best known today as the author of the hymn "Amazing Grace," and he is a central figure in the admired film of that name in theaters a few years ago, a powerful portrayal of him turning away from his devotion to the slave trade, in the 1780s. But

Newton evidently didn't have the grace to repent his devotion to contemptuous anti-Judaic sentiment.

Newton's *Discourses* may reasonably be taken to show how a great many early listeners will have understood Jennens and Handel's oratorio—his readings of Scripture were thoroughly standard fare both well before and well after *Messiah* was written. And with their conventionally disdainful views of Jews and Judaism, these *Messiah* sermons must also have long reinforced traditional understandings of Jennens's scripture compilation, seeing that Newton's sermons were frequently reprinted in the nineteenth and twentieth centuries.

We can learn still a bit more about Jennens and Psalm 2:9 by considering a manuscript poem of unknown authorship that was apparently owned by Jennens when he compiled his *Messiah* libretto. Under the title "*Verses 3–6 of a poem*," this manuscript is now housed in the Gerald Coke Handel Collection of the Foundling Museum in London. Part 4 of the poem, a paraphrase of Revelation 2:18–29, reads:

> To Thyatira's Angel write
> Thus doth the Son of God inspire,
> Whose eyes are like two flames of fire,
> Whose feet as polish'd brass are bright.
> Thy works well-pleas'd I see,
> Thy patience, faith & charity.
> But still a few things to thy charge I lay;
> Thou giv'st to Jezebel her way,
> And suff'rest that false prophetess
> In paths of vice & wickedness
> To lead my flock astray.
> Space for repentance she had giv'n,
> But still provokes the wrath of heav'n.

Behold I cast her in a bed of woe,

And anguish shall her followers undergo,

Unless repentance from instruction grow.

Her children will I kill with death,

And ev'ry church shall know

'Tis I who search the heart & reins

And joys or pains,

Bliss or woe

On all that breathe,

According to their works bestow.

But you who shun the sorc'ress' lore

Nor in the snares of Satan roam,

Still hold in goodness as before,

And wait in patience *'till I come.*

Who the conquest can obtain

O'er the nations he shall reign,

With iron rod, & unremitted blows,

Shall he persue the holy war,

In shivers like a potter's vessel break his foes;

And be rewarded with the morning star.

Let ev'ry ear

The Spirit's dictates to the churches hear. (my italics)

The key allusion for our purposes comes at the end of this excerpt from the poem, where the lines are based immediately on Revelation 2:24–28 and hence, at one remove, on Psalm 2:9. Verses
24–28 of Revelation 2 read: "But unto you [who are untainted by
false doctrine] I say, . . . hold fast *till I* [*Jesus*] *come.* . . . And he that
overcometh [i.e., the disciple of Jesus—a metonym for the Christian
Church—who overcomes, and keeps the Son of God's works], . . .
to him will I give power *over the nations:* (*He shall rule them* [the

unbelieving nations, that is, the gentiles and Jews] *with a rod of iron: as the vessels of a potter shall they be broken to shivers:*) even as I [the Son of God, Jesus] received of my Father. And I [Jesus] will give him [namely, the persevering victorious disciple, the church] the morning star [that is, I will give him my Self]" (my italics).

Concerning these verses from Revelation 2, Jennens's major source, Hammond, in *Paraphrase and Annotations upon all the Books of the New Testament*, writes: "[The fact] that [the talk of] the *coming of Christ* [Revelation 2:25] notes that notable destruction of his enemies—the Jewish crucifiers of *Christ*, and persecuters of Christians—hath often been showed (see [the author's comments on] Mat[thew].24.[endnote] b.). . . . [To those who had *not* fallen prey to false doctrine,] he [Jesus] gives no other counsel for the present, till this time come of destroying the Jewish persecuters and Judaizing *Gnostics*."

At Matthew 24, endnote b, then, Hammond explains that "this time" refers to the period of the Roman war against Judea in 66–73 CE, when God destroys Jerusalem and its Temple: "The *coming of Christ* is one of the phrases that is noted in this Book to signifie the Destruction of the Jews. . . . A threefold *coming of Christ* there is [to be understood in all]: 1. in the flesh, to be born among us; 2. At the day of Doom, to judge the world . . . 3. A middle coming, partly in vengeance, visible and observable on his enemies and Crucifiers, (and first on the people of the Jews . . .) and [partly] in mercy, to the relief of the persecuted Christians. . . . [An at least apparently reasonable objection is] that this Destruction [in 70 CE] being wrought by the Roman Army, and those [persons—the first-century Romans—having been] as much enemies of Christianity as any, and the very same people that had joyn'd with the Jews to put [Jesus] *Christ* to death, it doth appear strange, that either those Armies, which are call'd *abominable*, should be call'd God's Armies; or that

Christ should be said *to come*, when in truth it was *Vespasian* [from 66–69 CE, leader of the Roman army in the Jewish War; and from 69–79, emperor] and *Titus* [in the year 70, leader of the Roman army that destroyed Jerusalem and its Temple, and in the years 79–81, emperor] that thus came against this people ["the Jews"]. To this I answer, that 'tis ordinary with God in the Old Testament to call those *Babylonish*, *Assyrian*, heathen Armies, *his*, which did his work in punishing the Jews when they rebell'd against him. As for *Vespasian*, (though it need not be said, and though the answer is otherwise clear, that *Christ* is fitly said *to come* when his Ministers [i.e., God's agents of war; here, the Roman armies] do come, that is, when either heathen men or Satan himself, who are executioners of God's will when they think not of it, are permitted by him to work destruction on his enemies, to act revenge upon his Crucifiers) it is yet not unworthy of observation, how easie it might be in many particulars to shew that *Christ* was resembled or represented by that Emperour [Vespasian]."[19]

Psalm 2:9 is quoted not only at Revelation 2:24–28 but also at Revelation 12:5 and 19:15, in each case likewise apparently including Jews among "all nations [Greek, *ethnē*]" and among "the nations."[20] Revelation 12:5 reads in the King James Bible: "And she brought forth a man-child who was to rule *all nations* [i.e., the various heathen nations and the Jewish nation] with a rod of iron: and her child was caught up unto God, and to his throne."

The *she* of this verse has as its antecedent the woman of verse 1, which reads: "And there appeared a great wonder in heaven, a woman clothed with the sun, and the moon under her feet, and upon her head a crown of twelve stars."

In Protestant interpretations the *woman* of Revelation 12:1 was traditionally understood as luminous Ecclesia (Christianity), while "the moon under her feet" was understood as pale Synagoga

(Judaism). Wells, in *An Help for the More Easy and Clear Under-standing of the Holy Scriptures: Being the Revelation of St John the Divine* (1717), explains the standard view in this way: "[By Revelation 12:5] is denoted the Christian Church, adorn'd and shining with the Faith of Christ [Jesus] the Sun of Righteousness, and de-spising or casting off the Rites and Ceremonies of the Jewish Law, as what at least in reference to their Feasts directed by the Motion of the Moon, and also like the Moon was only a sort of reflected Light or a fainter and obscurer Revelation of the will of God and true Religion, and consequently was also, like the Moon, to have its Change or to last only for a season. And by the Crown of Twelve Stars is denoted the Rise of the Church."

Finally, the third quotation of Psalm 2:9 in the Book of Revelation, found at 19:15, reads in the King James Bible: "And out of his [i.e., from Christ's, the Word of God's] mouth goeth a sharp sword, that with it he should smite the nations [i.e., the Christ-denying Jewish and gentile nations]: and he shall rule them with a rod of iron: and he treadeth the wine-press of the fierceness and wrath of almighty God."

The Schadenfreude of the Hallelujah Chorus

So, what was the response in *Messiah* to Psalm 2's predicted vio-lence, in significant part, against the people of Israel; or, more spe-cifically, what was the immediate response to the words of an Old Testament text that was widely held as heralding, in part, the down-fall of Judaism and its replacement by Christianity? "Hallelujah! for the Lord God omnipotent reigneth. . . . *Hallelujah!*"

Here is the text of *Messiah* and its sources:

> *Jennens's* Messiah *Libretto*
> Hallelujah! for the Lord God omnipotent reigneth. The kingdom of this world is become the kingdom of our Lord and of his Christ;

and he shall reign for ever and ever, King of kings, and Lord of lords.
Hallelujah!

King James Bible, Revelation 19:6, 11:15, 19:16
<u>Alleluia</u>: for the Lord God omnipotent reigneth [19:6]. The <u>king-
doms</u> of this world <u>are</u> become the <u>kingdoms</u> of our Lord, and of his
Christ, and he shall reign for ever and ever [11:15]. KING OF KINGS,
AND LORD OF LORDS [19:16].

Wells, Revelation 19:6, 11:15, 19:16
Hallelujah; for the Lord God omnipotent reigneth [19:6]. The
kingdom of this world is become the kingdom of our Lord, and of his
Christ, and he shall reign for ever and ever [11:15]. KING OF KINGS,
AND LORD OF LORDS [19:16].

Wells explains that Revelation 11:15 concerns "[t]he happy state
of the Church upon the sounding of the seventh trumpet. . . . [T]he
supreme civil power here on earth is now in the hands of the saints
[i.e., the church] or faithful servants of [Jesus] Christ, . . . the saints
shall thus continue to have the dominion even of the earth to the
end of this world."

Jennens's influential source Hammond, however, in his *Paraphrase and Annotations upon all the Books of the New Testament*,
brings Psalm 2 yet more specifically to bear on the Revelation 11
passage's sense of Christian power—indeed, Jennens may have
taken the idea of juxtaposing these very passages from this book,
although there was in any event a long history of linking these two
passages (that is, of linking Psalm 2 with the *second* sentence of
the Hallelujah chorus, not the rejoicing first sentence). Hammond
writes extensively about calamities on "the Jews" at his comments
on Revelation 11:15 and following: "[paraphrase on Revelation
11:15] For as [the seventh Angel] sounded [the trumpet], thunders

were immediately heard, that is, pouring in of the Roman armies upon them, mentioned [at] verse 13; and an immense multitude of Jews, almost six hundred thousand of them, slain, saith [the Roman historian] Dio; others affirm as many more, from the beginning of this war. And as this was done on the seditious Jews, so by this means the Christians, especially of the Gentiles, came to flourish there more than ever, and the whole city became in a manner Gentile-Christian; . . . and thus the Church of Jerusalem entered upon her flourishing condition, and the faith of Christ got the upper hand. . . . [Paraphrase on the continuation at verse 18] Now is fulfilled that prophecy of Psalm 2. The Jewish nation have behaved themselves most stubbornly against [Jesus] Christ, and cruelly against Christians, and [God's] judgments are come upon them [with the wars of 66–73 and 132–35 CE]."

Hammond, highly unusually among pre-nineteenth-century Protestants, held that all or most predictions in the Book of Revelation were already fulfilled by the first and second centuries CE. His "preterist" view was opposed to the prevailing Protestant "historicist" view that these biblical predictions can be fulfilled all throughout the history of the church, even if mostly in the future, namely at the End Time.

And so, any proposed first-century fulfillments of predictions from the Book of Revelation are in principle acceptable to both a preterist like Hammond and a historicist like Matthew Henry, each of whom, as we saw, like *Messiah*, juxtaposes Psalm 2 to Revelation 11 (that is, 11:15 or 11:18). This mutual acceptability works because preterists reject only the historicist's prejudice for later-than-early-CE fulfillments, and because historicists reject only the preterist's prejudice against later-than-early-CE fulfillments.

Thus, for example, concerning Revelation 6:17, whose fulfillment many historicists placed in the End Time, Matthew Henry (via his redactors)[21] writes in his *Exposition of all the Books of the Old and New Testament*: "We have here the sixth Seal opened, [Revelation 6,] *v*[*erse*]. 12. Some refer this to the great Revolutions in the Empire in *Constantine*'s Time, the Downfall of Paganism; others, with great probability, to the Destruction of *Jerusalem*, as an Emblem of the General Judgment, and Destruction of the Wicked at the end of the World. And indeed the awful Characters of this Event are so much the same with those Signs mentioned by our Saviour, as foreboding the Destruction of *Jerusalem*, that it hardly leaves any room for doubting but that the same thing is meant in both places; tho' some think that Event was past already. See *Matth*[*ew*]. xxiv.29,30. Here observe, . . . The Destruction of the *Jewish* Nation should affect and affright all the Nations round about: Those that were highest in Honour, and those that seemed to be best secured. It would be a Judgment that should astonish all the World. . . . All these Terrors actually fell upon the Sinners in *Judea* and *Jerusalem* in the Day of their Destruction, and they will all, in the utmost degree, fall upon impenitent Sinners, at the General Judgment of the Last Day."

At the time Jennens was compiling his *Messiah* libretto, the preterist approach to Scripture remained very much out of favor among Protestants. The commentaries of Hammond were nonetheless widely cited with approval in the eighteenth century by non-preterists (like Matthew Henry), doubtless because so many of his biblical insights were in fact not incompatible with a historicist approach.

In any event, for present purposes, it doesn't matter whether the texts from Revelation 11 and 19 in *Messiah* have to do with the past or the future. Either way, as a response to the import of Psalm 2 as it is to be read in light of Acts 4, the Hallelujah chorus is rejoicing in part against Jews and Judaism. Both for secular ethics and for biblical ethics this represents a special and serious problem, an issue I'll address in appropriate detail at the conclusion of this essay.

Concerning the "King of kings, and Lord of lords" (Revelation 19:16, quoted at the final section of the Hallelujah chorus), Pearson, in his *Exposition of the Creed* (1659), another well-known book owned by Jennens (in an edition of 1710, as mentioned earlier), and for 250 years a standard text for ordinands in the Church of England, writes: "*King of kings, and Lord of lords* (Rev[elation]. 19.16). . . . [Jesus Christ] showeth his Regal Dominion in the destruction of his enemies, whether they were temporal or spiritual enemies. Temporal, as the *Jews* and *Romans*, who joined together in his Crucifixion. While he was on earth he told his disciples (Mat[thew]. 16.28), *There be some standing here which shall not taste of death till they see the son of man coming in his kingdom*: and in that kingdom he was then seen to come, when [in the years 66–73] he brought utter destruction on the *Jews* by the *Roman* Armies. . . . Thus [in destroying his *temporal* enemies, including "the Jews" and, eventually, pagans; as well as also his *spiritual* enemies, including, in the end, Sin and Death] is our *Jesus* become the *Prince of the kings of the earth*; thus is the *Lamb* [God's messiah, Jesus] acknowledged to be *Lord of lords, and King of kings* (Rev[elation] 1.5 and 17.14)."

I register here, following on Pearson's talk of the Romans and Jews, my puzzlement with people who've told me that Jennens's sources and libretto cannot properly be called disdainful toward Judaism because these various texts speak explicitly or implicitly against not only those Jews who don't believe in Jesus but also the pagan Romans. Consider, however, for the moment—other considerations will follow—this response: what should one make, for example, of white South African advocates of racial apartheid who said they could not justly be labeled "antiblack," seeing that they wished to be kept apart not only from the Bantu but also from the Indian and Pakistani populations in their country?

Readers may wonder what additional contributions, however slight, Handel's music for the Hallelujah chorus might make to our story of anti-Judaic schadenfreude. In this chorus the general mood is one of spectacular triumph. It's at the Hallelujah chorus that trumpets with drums are used for the first time in *Messiah*.[22] In Handel's day trumpets with drums were symbols of great power. Listen to the way they're used in baroque opera: brass with drums are scored in music for *winners*. In *Messiah*, trumpets with drums contribute dramatically to celebrating the destruction of Christ's "enemies" that had been prefigured in Psalm 2.

The eighteenth-century English music historian Charles Burney, in his *An Account of the Musical Performances in Westminster-Abbey, and the Pantheon . . . 1784: In Commemoration of Handel* (1785), writes of the Hallelujah chorus: "The opening is clear, cheerful, and bold. And the words, 'For the Lord God omnipotent reigneth,' (Rev[elation] xix.6.) [are] set to a fragment of *canto fermo* [a preexisting melody, taken from a hymn tune or Gregorian chant], which all the parts sing, as such, in unisons and octaves, has an effect truly ecclesiastical [that is, church-like]. It is afterwards made the subject of fugue [a kind of music in which the voices more or less imitate one another melodically] and ground-work for the Allelujah."

As Tassilo Erhardt has argued in his recent book *Händels Messiah*, the melody in question corresponds subtly to the Lutheran chorale "Wie schön leuchtet der Morgenstern" of Phillip Nicolai, where the setting of the words "Mein König und mein Bräutigam" lines up musically with Handel's "For the Lord God omnipotent reigneth." Handel would naturally have known the Lutheran repertory of church hymns from his German childhood.

An English version (not well known to Handel's contemporaries) of Nicolai's chorale appeared in the *Lyra Davidica* (1708) as "How Fairly Shines ye Morning Star":

> How fairly shines ye morning star,
> with grace & truth beyond compare,
> great Jesse's offspring royal.
> Hail David's son of Jacob's line,
> thou art my king & spouse divine,
> thou hast my heart true loyal.
> Lovely, kind, free,
> in whose sweet face, celestial grace
> in full glory
> shines from heaven's highest story.

A more triumphal version appears in the *Psalmodia Germanica; or, The German Psalmody* (1732), a collection—dedicated to the (German-born) Prince of Wales and his wife—that grew out of the usage of the German Royal Chapel at St. James's Palace:

> How bright appears the Morning-Star,
> With Grace and Truth beyond Compare,
> The Royal Root of JESSE;
> O *David*'s Son, of *Jacob*'s Line!
> My Soul's Delight, and Spouse Divine,
> Thy love can only bless me.
> Precious, Gracious,
> Fair and Glorious, e'r Victorious,
> Thou my Treasure,
> Far beyond all earthly Pleasure.

Reasonable people can certainly differ on whether this melodic setting of Handel's for the words "For the Lord God omnipotent reigneth" truly alludes to the internal rising four-note and falling four-note melodic idea from the hymn "Wie schön leuchtet."

For one thing, that musical idea appears much more straightforwardly in a number of Handel's choruses from other works: for example—as John Roberts has pointed out in a recent article[23]—at "I will sing unto the Lord" in *Israel in Egypt*,[24] at the closing movements of the "Utrecht Te Deum," and at certain versions of the anthem "Let God Arise." Are any or all of these slow-motion rising and falling four-note scalar patterns allusions to "Wie schön leuchtet"? They might well be.

Roberts's article also calls attention to a very close musical correspondence between bars 12–14 from the Hallelujah chorus and an instrumental fugue attributed to the great Italian composer and acquaintance of Handel's, Arcangelo Corelli (1653–1713). Roberts's article goes on to report that this instrumental fugue also bears similarity to a main theme from Corelli's Concerto in D Major, op. 6, no. 1.

On the face of it, this all does sound like a good argument. But under scrutiny, problems arise. First, the fugue survives in only a single manuscript copy (which is not in Corelli's handwriting), where for some reason the composer is identified as Gallario Riccoleno, apparently an anagram for "Arcangiolo Corelli" (*Arcangiolo* being Florentine dialect for *Arcangelo*). The music remained unpublished until it appeared within a late-twentieth-century scholarly compilation of the complete works of Corelli. There the piece is found not in the main text with Corelli's canonical works but in the appendix, which is titled "Doubtful Works, a Selection." Although in his critical commentaries the editor describes the Corellian authenticity of the fugue as "supposable" or even "very likely," he nonetheless opts not to incorporate the music into the Corelli canon. Handel's having known the fugue isn't impossible (whoever its composer was), but the more obscure the provenance and authorship of the piece, the less likely Handel is to have been familiar with it.

A second problem is that although the Corelli concerto theme is musically somewhat close to the Riccoleno fugue theme and the Riccoleno fugue theme is musically very close to the Handel chorus theme, the bona fide Corelli concerto theme is musically not very close to the Handel chorus theme.

If A is a bit like B, and B is very much like C, it doesn't follow that A is a lot like C. What we appear to have here is not two Corelli antecedents but simply one perhaps-Corelli correspondence.

This close correspondence of the setting of "For the Lord God omnipotent reigneth" in the Hallelujah chorus with the obscure Riccoleno fugue—of B with C—might well be coincidental.[25] Certainly, the question of what Charles Burney meant when he said these words were "set to a fragment of *canto fermo*" needs to be considered. Did he mean to convey that Handel's melodic idea was *like* a hymn tune or Gregorian chant, or did he mean that it *was* such a thing? Whatever the answer might be, Burney most likely was not thinking of an instrumental fugue attributed to Gallario Riccoleno. (This isn't to say, however, that Burney must have been right in suggesting that Handel was setting a fragment of cantus firmus.)

Perhaps the simpler and more plausible solution, after all, is to consider the Hallelujah chorus theme in the context of Lutheran hymnody, music with which Handel was familiar from his Lutheran upbringing in Germany and from his later keeping abreast of German church music.

At bar 34 and following from the Hallelujah chorus, there is a more striking quotation from another Nicolai chorale, "Wachet auf, ruft uns die Stimme." Handel's music employs a particular melodic fragment from the chorale twice in a row, first to the words

"The kingdom of this world" and then instrumentally. An English version of this second Nicolai chorale also appeared in the *Lyra Davidica*, as "Awake ye Voice is Crying":

> Awake ye voice is crying
> o' the watchmen from their towers espying,
> O wake O city of Jerusalem.
> 'Tis midnight cry surrounding
> while clear and shrill ye voice is sounding,
> haste virgins decked with Wisdom's sacred gem.
> Now comes your spouse & king,
> love's burning lamps now bring.
> Halleluja;
> get ready trimmed & dressed for the nuptial feast
> and haste to welcome down your Lordly guest.

And at bar 41 and following there is a second quotation from "Wachet auf": Handel's fugue melody for the words "and he shall reign for ever and ever" is loosely but, for those who know "Wachet auf," recognizably based on the hymn tune.

Why quote chorales, and why from the thousands of Lutheran hymns these two? I very much doubt that many of Handel's original listeners were clued in to any such allusions, except perhaps for some members of the ruling Hanoverian (that is, Lutheran-born and German-speaking) royal family and their German courtiers. If these were indeed conscious hymn quotations, Handel may of course have had personal reasons that we can't divine. Or were they Jennens's suggestion?

Whatever answers there may be to the biographical question concerning why Handel's music is the way it is, however, the question I want to pursue is the interpretive one: what does Handel's music mean when it is the way it apparently is?

Once anyone has noticed, or has been made aware of, these two chorale correspondences in the Hallelujah chorus, what can one reasonably take their presence to signify? Where they are specifically placed within part 2 of *Messiah*, I see the two chorales making possible a slight heightening of the chorus's already altogether-vigorous Christian rejoicing against Judaism.

Both Nicolai hymns use biblical language from the story in Matthew 25:1–13 of the Wise and Foolish Virgins: Ten virgins are waiting for the bridegroom to come. The foolish virgins don't have enough oil in their lamps to last until midnight, when the bridegroom arrives. They've gone off in search of more oil, and thus miss the arrival of the groom. When they come to the marriage feast the door is shut. The bridegroom rejects them, saying, "Verily I say unto you, I know you not."

Biblical interpreters generally agree that Matthew 25:1–13 is a parable about the future Second Coming of Christ. Jesus, the bridegroom, will marry his bride, the Christian Church, in a great heavenly feast, an event that some invited guests will be in a position to attend and others won't.

The text isn't always clear on whether the Foolish Virgins simply represent all the unsaved or a particular group that personifies, as it were, and acts as emblematic of the unsaved. One inveterate tradition, still frequently preached in certain circles today, is that the five Wise Virgins are to be associated with eternally saved Ecclesia (the church, Christianity), while the Foolish Virgins are to be associated with eternally rejected Synagoga (the synagogue, Judaism).

Whether Jennens had any hand in Handel's compositional choices in the Hallelujah chorus is unknown. He seems to have had a musical influence elsewhere in *Messiah* (as indicated, for example, in his letter of 30 August 1745 to an unspecified addressee), most notably in his apparent insistence that Handel write a powerful chorus to replace a solo aria setting of "Their Sound is gone out into all Lands" (such that Handel composed the choral movement now listed as no. 39 in *Messiah* to substitute for the final section of the aria that is listed as no. 38b).

Jennens was extremely well informed about art, theology, and biblical interpretation, and he will almost certainly have read, for example, the pitiless Ecclesia against Synagoga interpretation of Matthew 25, associated expressly with the first-century destruction of Jerusalem, in one of Samuel Clarke's major theological works, *A Paraphrase on the Four Evangelists . . . Very useful for Families* (1736). (Clarke was an extremely influential author and is well represented in Jennens's library.) Also, for centuries many cathedral sculptures, stained glass, and altar paintings had specifically linked a triumphant Ecclesia with the Wise Virgins and a broken, abject Synagoga with the Foolish Virgins.[26]

Handel's use of Nicolai's "Wachet auf" in the Hallelujah chorus may, too, in part have been verbally triggered: at the hymn's first stanza the response to the Wise Virgins' preparing soon to meet the bridegroom is "Hallelujah!"

The Hallelujah chorus in and of itself need not, of course, be taken to project Christian rejoicing, even in part, against Judaism. The context in which the chorus appears makes all the difference. Handel, for example, reused this movement in the late 1740s in his *Anthem for the Foundling Hospital*, where it follows upon various Psalm texts celebrating God's care for the needy. Where it is originally situated in *Messiah*, however, the Hallelujah chorus gathers a significant confrontational force from its direct juxtaposition to *stile concitato* settings of a Psalm text that was conventionally understood in the eighteenth century (and also later) to predict, in part, God's destruction of Jerusalem and its Temple because of Jewish failure to accept Jesus as God's messiah.

In *Messiah*, the Hallelujah chorus can already powerfully express its anti-Judaism whether or not one notices or accepts its possible chorale allusions. It's worth noting, in any event, that if the Hallelujah chorus's hymn references indeed help project an even-greater rejoicing against Judaism in *Messiah* than what is already provided in abundance just by dint of this chorus text and its general musical setting's having come right after settings of Psalm 2, the hymns certainly do nothing at all to suggest exultation over the breaking or dashing to pieces of any Roman or other gentile institutions.

To be clearer yet, though, on the issue of Christianity's "enemies," one might reasonably wonder, If Handel's *Messiah*, taken as a whole, indeed expresses any triumphal Christian rejoicing against Judaism, doesn't it project the very same attitude correspondingly toward *all* populations who don't believe in Jesus? Can and should *Messiah*'s rejoicing against Judaism be understood, within this perspective, as a *special* problem?

The answer is yes. Historically, Christian triumphing over Judaism has played out rather differently than its triumphing over paganism, Islam, and other cultural-religious traditions. Notably, Christians' violence against Jews—to cite only several examples: the eleventh-century First Crusade, the fifteenth-century expulsion from Spain, and the extensive direct and indirect complicity in the twentieth-century murder of millions[27]—was against civilians. The pagans, Muslims, and others—like Christians but *not* Jews after the first century CE—typically had armies.

Apparently less well known (or perhaps ignored), however, and well worth calling attention to, is the fact that for Jennens's intended Christian audience, and therefore for any historically informed study of *Messiah*, there is another reason Christian rejoicing against Judaism should be understood as a special problem:

such rejoicing is contrary to the spirit—and in all probability to the letter—of a (highly specific) directive of the New Testament. At Romans 11:17–18a the apostle Paul writes: "But if some of the branches were broken [on the cultivated olive tree, a metaphor for the family of God, with the *broken* branches representing those Jews among Israel who do not believe in Jesus] and you [gentile follower of Jesus], being a [shoot from a] wild olive tree, were grafted in among them and became a joint sharer of the root of the richness of the [cultivated] olive tree [i.e., such that the broken but protectively 'callused' branches are still drawing nourishment from the root], *do not rejoice/self-boast against the branches* [Greek: *mē katakauchō tōn kladōn*]."[28]

This passage from the Book of Romans—written by Paul from his perspective as "an Israelite, . . . of the tribe of Benjamin" (Romans 11:1)—thus warns against gentile Christian condescension toward historical Israel generally (that is, toward Jews who believe in Jesus, as well as toward Jews who don't). For present purposes, though, the aspect of Romans 11 that bears highlighting might be paraphrased as follows: "You gentile believer in Jesus: do not exult over, or feel self-pride in the face of, any misfortune experienced by those Jews who do not believe in Jesus."

Jennens (and Handel) may have missed or ignored Paul's concerns here about unbelievers in Jesus among historical Israel,[29] but their significance was not lost, for example, on a leading eighteenth-century biblical interpreter like Matthew Henry, who, in his *Exposition of all the Books of the Old and New Testament*, writes (via his redactors) specifically of these sentiments at Romans 11: "[Christians] must not insult and triumph over those poor *Jews* [i.e., the *temporarily* broken 'branches'—see verses 23, 26, and 28–29 of Romans 11], but rather pity them, and desire their Welfare, and long for the receiving of them in again."[30]

It's worth noting, too, that while the New Testament often projects a remarkable severity when speaking of Jews who do not believe in Jesus,[31] there are no scriptural texts that counter Romans 11 by suggesting that Christian schadenfreude against Judaism is meet or salutary at any time and in any place. Of course the Psalms are revered as part of Christian scripture, and many of the Psalms rejoice in the destruction of the enemies of God's covenant people. But if one determines from this that it is therefore biblically right or fitting for Christians to rejoice against Judaism, then he or she presumes, against Romans 9–11, that Jews are not biblically God's covenant people.[32]

From the standpoint of Paul's directive regarding the peculiar problem of gentile Christian attitudes toward Jewish unbelievers in Jesus, an objection that the Hallelujah chorus also exults over or expresses gratitude for the dashing to pieces of gentile nations who don't believe in Jesus would be beside the point.[33] Both for secular and for biblical ethics, Christian rejoicing against Judaism is a special, and morally urgent, problem.

Whether or not one accepts that Psalm 2 is to be understood in part as prefiguring specifically the destruction of Jerusalem and its Temple, the Hallelujah chorus is nevertheless undeniably a joyous utterance following directly upon movements that are to be understood prophetically to speak, in significant part, of some fierce ruin or another for "the people [*of Israel*]," "the Jews." We know this because Psalm 2:9 and 2:1, in the traditional (typological) theological world of *Messiah*, are meant to be read in light of the New Testament glossing of Psalm 2:1 at Acts 4:25–29, where Psalm 2's "the people" is specifically identified as Jesus-threatening ethnic Israel; thus the words "of Israel" are supposed to be read into Jennens's libretto.

And so allow me to present the following question clearly and most emphatically: *To conclude that the Hallelujah chorus involves anti-Judaic rejoicing, need one come up with any more persuasive evidence than that in* Messiah *Psalm 2 is meant to be read in light of its use in Acts 4?*

If a chorus gives expression to *any* joy or gratitude right after the libretto's reference to the dashing to pieces of a "them" that includes Jews, then that choral number—whether intentionally or not, and whether naturally picked up and endorsed by listeners or not—is effectively disobeying Paul's instruction for Christians not to rejoice and/or self-boast against Judaism.

Given that the particular biblical, theological, and historical relationships of the Christian Church to Jewish unbelievers in Jesus are fundamentally different from those of the church to gentile unbelievers, the very act of rejoicing in any form by New Israel over any sort of ruin experienced by so-called Old Israel inherently and essentially involves a kind of self-exaltation. This entails the vaunting of assumed superiority by a mere grafted shoot from a wild olive tree over and against the natural branches from the cultivated olive tree, even if the joy expressed does not feature verbally explicit self-boasting.

Some eminent readers of an earlier draft of this book have told me that in the end my rereading of *Messiah* strikes them as unconvincing because, they say, it rests on one small textual change and the placement of the Hallelujah chorus next to Psalm 2. But—leaving aside the problem of whether it's true that the rereading rests on those two things (in fact, it's obviously untrue)—consider the following: If Psalm 2 here prophetically refers to the ruin, in part, of Jews and if the immediate response to the destruction is "Hallelujah!" then how on earth can the notion that Handel's *Messiah* rejoices, in part, against Judaism justly seem unconvincing? What further proof would you need?

Another Instructive Polemical Example
in Handel with Paired Hymn Tunes

Is there even one additional work by Jennens and Handel in which the expression of contempt for other religious traditions features as a significant aspect? It should come as no surprise that, yes, there is.

Not long before *Messiah*, Jennens and Handel collaborated on the moral cantata *L'allegro, il penseroso ed il moderato*. Its closing chorus, "Thy Pleasures, Moderation, Give," likewise features musical allusions to two Lutheran hymns. The full text of Jennens's chorus reads:

> Thy pleasures, *Moderation*, give;
> in them alone we truly live.

Handel set these words to the opening musical phrases of the famous Lutheran chorale "Jesu, meine Freude." This was probably verbally prompted by Jennens's word *pleasures*. Handel's inclusion of the melody from "Jesu, meine Freude," then, may locate the source of one's true pleasure in God's messiah, Jesus. In the *Psalmodia Germanica* (1732) the text of the first verse reads:

> Jesu! source of gladness,
> comfort in my sadness,
> thou canst end my grief;
> Lord, thy sight I'm wanting,
> while my heart is panting,
> after thy relief.
> Saviour Christ! my Lamb and Priest!

heaven and earth, without thy treasure,

can afford no pleasure.

Later in this cantata chorus, just like in the Hallelujah chorus, a second Lutheran chorale is musically quoted, and here, as there, it's for a fugue subject. This time Handel employs Luther's infamous polemical hymn "Erhalt uns, Herr, bei deinem Wort."

Orthodox Lutherans of Handel's day sang the first lines of this chorale to these words:

Erhalt uns, Herr, bei deinem Wort
Und steur des Papsts und Türken Mord,
Die Jesum Christum, deinen Sohn,
Stürzen wollen von seinem Thron!

("Uphold us, Lord, with your word,

and restrain the murderousness of the Pope and the Turk [that is,

'the Muslim'],

who want to topple Jesus Christ,

your Son, from his throne!")

This is the text used, for example, in the opening chorus from J. S. Bach's musically magnificent Cantata 126.[34]

The hymn "Erhalt uns, Herr" was well known to Jennens's and Handel's English contemporaries, for example, from its inclusion at the end of the constantly reprinted Sternhold and Hopkins metrical psalter. (It was sung to the tune quoted by Handel.) Here's the text of the hymn, as printed in 1730 in Thomas Sternhold and John Hopkins, *The Whole Book of Psalms: Collected into English Metre*:[35]

Preserve us, Lord, by thy dear word,

from Turk and Pope defend us, Lord:

both which would thrust out of his throne
our Lord, Christ Jesus, thy dear Son.

Lord Jesus Christ, shew us thy might,
that thou art Lord of lords by right:
thy poor afflicted flock defend,
that we may praise thee without end.

God, holy Ghost, the Comforter,
be our patron, help, and succour:
give us one mind, and perfect peace,
all gifts of grace in us increase.

Thou living God in persons three,
thy name be prais'd in unity:
in all our need so us defend,
that we may praise thee without end.

The inclusion of this hymn melody in Handel's chorus affords the notion that "we [proper, Protestant Christian believers] *truly live*" if God will "preserve us" from, among other immoderate things, the horrors of Islam and Roman Catholicism.[36]

To be sure, I'm not claiming that this is the main focus or the entire message of Jennens and Handel's chorus, but I am suggesting it's a nontrivial aspect of its meaning.

TWO REMAINING KEY PASSAGES

At several individual key places in *Messiah* we might misconstrue the overall meaning of the oratorio if we don't read its Old Testament passages in light of how they're used in the New Testament; that is to say, we'll misunderstand *Messiah* if we fail to read these biblical allusions and quotations prophetically or typologically.

Nos. 27 to 28 in *Messiah* are settings of Psalm 22:7–8, which appear in the Old Testament as a part of a poem of King David's lamenting the derisive behavior of his enemies. David's words are applied to the crucified Jesus, however, in the New Testament at Matthew 27:39–43, where, according to the biblical thinking that *Messiah*'s libretto is premised upon, the words of Psalm 22 must achieve their true meaning.

Compare the Psalm with *Messiah* and with Matthew:

> *King James Bible*, Psalm 22:7–8
>
> All they that see me [David, the type; Jesus, the antitype] laugh me to scorn: they shoot out the lip, they shake the head, saying, "He trusted on the LORD, that he would deliver him: let him deliver him, seeing he delighted in him" (*margin*, "Or, '*if he delight in him*')."

> *Book of Common Prayer*, Psalm 22:7–8
>
> All they that see me [David, the type; Jesus, the antitype], laugh me to scorn: they shoot out their lips, and shake their heads, saying, "He trusted in God, that he would deliver him: let him deliver him, if he will have him."

> *Jennens's* Messiah *Libretto*
>
> All they that see him [Jesus, the antitype] laugh him to scorn; they shoot out their Lips, and shake their Heads, saying, "he trusted in God, that He would deliver him: Let Him deliver him, if He delight in him."

> *King James Bible*, Matthew 27:39–40,43
>
> And they [the Jewish pilgrims attending Passover] that passed by [Jesus, on the cross], reviled him, wagging their heads, and saying, "Thou that destroyest the temple, and buildest it in three days [see Matthew 26:61], save thyself. If thou be the Son of God, come down from the cross." [And the leaders of "the people"—"the Jews"—

likewise exclaim mockingly:] "he trusted in God; let Him deliver him now, if He will have him."

So when the *Messiah* libretto says at no. 27, "All *they* that see him laugh him to scorn," it cannot be referring to all sinful humanity. The followers of Jesus in Matthew 27, for example, certainly did not laugh him to scorn. Indeed, it's virtually unimaginable that any follower of Jesus would ever do so, then or at any later time. And though there were of course Romans too who "see"—in the historical-present tense—Jesus on the cross, it is readily understood in the Gospel of Matthew, and thus to be understood in *Messiah*, that no heathen would ever speak the words of the libretto's narratively adjoining movement, no. 28, "he [Jesus] trusted in God, that He [God] would deliver him [from the cross]: Let Him deliver him, if He [takes] delight in him."

Charles Burney, in his *An Account of the Musical Performances in Westminster-Abbey*, writes of this chorus: "The words of [Handel's] admirable choral fugue: '*He trusted in God that he would deliver him; let him deliver him, if he delight in him*' (Matth[hew] xxvii.43. and Psal[m] xxii.8.)—which contain the triumphal insolence, and are prophetic of the contumelious language of the Jews, during the crucifixion of our Saviour—were very difficult to express [musically]; however, HANDEL, availing himself in the most masterly manner of the advantage of fugue and imitation, has given them the effect, not of the taunts and presumption of an individual, but the scoffs and scorn of a confused multitude." (Burney is, I assume, echoing here the words of Lord Talbot in Shakespeare's *The First Part of King Henry the Sixth*, act 1, scene 4, lines 39–41: "With *scoffs and scorns* and *contumelious taunts*, in open marketplace produced they me, to be a public spectacle to all.")

In summary, at Matthew 27 all those who deride Jesus on the cross are Jewish pilgrims attending Passover, and this is certainly not a matter of, as it were, "all humanity" (that is, including Christians), laughing God's messiah to scorn.

Similarly, when Jennens's libretto states at no. 26, "All we, like Sheep, have gone astray . . . and the Lord [God] hath laid on him [Jesus] the Iniquity of us all," it isn't trying to make all humanity accountable as actual or potential deniers of Jesus. Whatever this text from Isaiah 53:6 might otherwise be taken to mean, according to traditional Christian readings of the Old Testament—that is, again, according to the approaches that *Messiah*'s libretto is premised upon—the true meaning of Isaiah 53:6 is to be governed by the way this passage is quoted in the New Testament, namely at 1 Peter 2:21–25. Peter is addressing *believers in Jesus* who have gone astray and *are healed* (that is, "saved") by Christ. The full passage reads: "Christ [Jesus] also suffered for us, leaving us [who are not the unbelievers in him (the "them who are disobedient")—1 Peter 2:7—but who are, rather, his followers (the "you which believe")—1 Peter 1, verses 2–10, 12–18, 20–22, and 25; 1 Peter 2, verses 2–3, 5, 7, 9, 11–13, 15–16, 18, 20–21, and 24–25] an example, that ye [his followers] should follow his steps. . . . [Christ Jesus] who, when he was reviled [on the cross, by *them*, the unbelievers in him], reviled not again [in return against them]; . . . who his own self bore our sins in his own body on the tree [i.e., the cross], [in order] that we [his followers], being dead to sins, should live unto righteousness: *by whose stripes* [i.e., bodily blood-welts] *ye* [his followers] *were healed*. For *ye were as sheep going astray*; but [because the Lord God has laid on him, Jesus, the iniquity of us all, the iniquity of all Jesus' sheep, of his followers, namely by ordaining Jesus' sacrificial death on the cross, you, his followers] are now returned unto the Shepherd and Bishop of your souls."

So how does this play out in *Messiah*? Nos. 26 and 27 do clearly put forward a strong verbal juxtaposition: a rather cheery, upbeat "all *we*" followed by a ferocious "all *they*."

The different musical styles in Handel's setting powerfully reinforce this textual *us*-against-*them* contrast, where Isaiah 53 and 1 Peter 2's "all *we* [i.e., Christians] . . . have gone astray . . . and with his Stripes *we* [Christians] are healed" is opposed to Psalm 22 and Matthew 27's "all *they* ['the Jews'] that see him laugh him [Jesus] to scorn . . . He [Jesus] trusted in God, that He would deliver him: Let Him deliver him, if He delight in him."

The chorus "And with his Stripes we are healed" is set exclusively in the *stylus ecclesiasticus*, the "church style," a traditional musical language, reminiscent of the great renaissance composer Giovanni Pierluigi da Palestrina (c. 1525–94), in which all the lines in the texture are melodic in character, featuring staggered imitative entries of "vocal melody" (as opposed to the kinds of melody that are idiomatic to instruments, like the violin) and a strict avoidance of dance rhythms.

The chorus "He trusted in God, that He would deliver him: Let Him deliver him, if He delight in him," by contrast, is set in the aggressive style of so-called *turba* choruses, the more turbulent "crowd" numbers that are found in contemporaneous baroque musical settings of the passion narrative. This is the style employed, for example, when the chorus of Jews in Bach's *St. Matthew Passion* exclaims, "Er hat Gott vertrauet, der erlöse ihn nun, lüstets ihn" ("He trusted in God—who may redeem him now, should He desire him"), and also when *das Volk* ("the people"—Luther's misrendering of Matthew's expression "the [ethnically mixed] crowds") shout out concerning Jesus, "Laß ihn kreuzigen!" ("Have him crucified!").

It appears, then, that Jennens's text and Handel's music at nos. 27 to 28 are designed here not merely to narrate indirectly several events from the passion narrative in the Gospel of Matthew. These movements form part of an "all-they" contrast with the "all-we" of the preceding nos. 24 to 26. In the context of *Messiah*, what the oratorio's listeners have—to put it starkly—is a placing of (hostile) Jews against (saved) Christians.[37]

CALLING HANDEL A "JEW" (IN THE EIGHTEENTH CENTURY)

Some of my fellow *Messiah* enthusiasts have claimed that we have good external evidence suggesting that Jennens may in fact have been a *philo*-semite. For the present study, this is a significant, potentially damning claim. Would a pro-Judaic librettist, intentionally or unintentionally, produce an anti-Judaic libretto?

So, what is this pro-Judaic evidence then, and how good is it?

Leading Handel scholar Ruth Smith, of Cambridge University, provides the details, writing in her *New York Times* essay from 25 April 2007, "Ruth Smith on Handel's 'Messiah'": "Neither Jennens nor Handel left any anti-Judaic remark. *On the contrary*. When Jennens complained to his friend [the Virgil scholar] Edward Holdsworth [1684–1746] that Handel had not done justice to all the texts of 'Messiah,' Holdsworth replied: 'I am sorry to hear yr. friend Handel is such a Jew. [An ellipsis that is needed does not appear here.] I hope the words, tho' murther'd, are still to be seen.' Jennens replied: 'You do him too much Honour to call him a Jew! A Jew would have paid more respect to the Prophets'" (my italics).

Jennens's reply, however, is assuredly *not* the opposite of an anti-Judaic remark. (And I frankly don't see that Jennens even tempers Holdsworth's remark at all.)

It's worth reading the letters more fully and carefully. Holdsworth had written to Jennens: "I am sorry to hear yʳ friend Handel is such a jew. His negligence [in setting *Messiah*], to say no worse, has been a great disappointment to others as well as yʳ self, for I hear there was great expectation of his composition. I hope the words, tho' murther'd, are still to be seen, and yᵗ [that] I shall have that pleasure [of simply reading your libretto] when I return [to England from France]. And as I don't understand the musick I shall be better off than the rest of yᵉ [the] world."

Jennens replied: "Last Friday Handel perform'ᵈ his [oratorio] Samson, a most exquisite Entertainment; which tho' I heard with infinite Pleasure, yet it increas'ᵈ my resentment for his [interpretive] neglect of the [libretto that I compiled for his oratorio] Messiah. You do him too much Honour to call him a Jew! a Jew would have paid more respect to the Prophets. The Name of Heathen will suit him better. Yet a sensible Heathen would not have prefer'ᵈ the Nonsense, foisted by one [Newburgh] Hamilton [c. 1692–1761] into Milton's Samson Agonistes, to the sublime Sentiments & expressions of Isaiah & David, of the Apostles & Evangelists; & of Jesus Christ."[38]

As revealed by this exchange, Holdsworth and Jennens (rhetorically) consider Handel to have behaved as badly as, or worse than, a Jew (who, by traditional Christian definition, is partly Godless). And Jennens descends farther, considering him even worse than a heathen (who, by traditional Christian definition, is wholly Godless).

Jennens's response warrants still further discussion, seeing that several of my eminent scholarly colleagues have maintained (on the internet discussion list Handel-L, initially founded by the American Handel Society) that Jennens shifts the discourse away from Holdsworth's jocularity against Jews and instead replies with seriousness about—my italics—"the respect Jews have *for scripture*."

Now, for a start, Jennens plainly does *not* reverse the discourse by moving from Holdsworth's pejorative, jocular use of the word

Jew to a nonpejorative, serious use. Rather, he does nothing to counter Holdsworth's jocular vein, speaking in fact not of the great respect Jews pay, but of the greater respect that (even) a Jew would have paid, to the Prophets; and Jennens goes on doing nothing to counter his friend's jocular vein, speaking of how not even a heathen would conduct himself with such immoderate negligence as Handel has done.

Furthermore, Jennens here speaks not generally of "Scripture" but specifically of "the Prophets." The difference is crucial to a valid understanding of his response. For Jennens, Scripture consisted of an Old Testament (whose sources are in Hebrew, with some Aramaic) containing the Law and the Prophets,[39] and various other books;[40] of an Apocrypha (in Greek); and of a New Testament (in Greek) containing the Gospels, and the Epistles, and the Apocalypse.

Observant Jews who are unbelievers in Jesus, of course, do not respect the New Testament as Scripture. They venerate the older, Hebrew materials, officially calling them not the Old Testament but Tanakh. Jewish Scripture consists of Torah (the Teaching), Nevi'im (the Prophets), and Kethuvim (the Writings)—hence the word *Tanakh*, an acronym based on the letters *T*, *N*, and *K*.

Needless to say, these Jews interpret the books of their Bible, the Tanakh, differently from how Christians interpret the same books from the Old Testament of their Bible. For Christians the most significant disagreements with Jewish interpretations concern the Prophets, as these are the books that Christians rely on the most heavily in their conviction that Jesus of Nazareth was the messiah of God foretold in Hebrew Scripture.

Traditional Christian writers of Jennens's day shared the view that among the books common to the Jewish and the Christian Bibles, the group of books that post-Jesus Jews most profoundly misinterpret, and perilously undervenerate, is the Prophets. Indeed, in this view a Jew who has praiseworthy veneration for the Prophets would forsake Judaism and acknowledge, out of creditable respect for ancient biblical prophecy, that Jesus of Nazareth was God's messiah.

Consider here the relevant key New Testament passage of John 5:39–40, where Jesus says to "the Jews," as rendered in the King James Bible, "Search the scriptures; for in them ye think ye have eternal life: and they are they which testify of me [as God's messiah]. And ye will not come to me, that ye might have [eternal] life." Matthew Henry, in his *Exposition of all the Books of the Old and New Testament*, notes concerning this passage, "[Jesus] annexeth a Reproof of [the Jews'] Infidelity and Wickedness . . . particularly, 1. Their *Neglect of him* and his Doctrine, [John 5,] *v*[*erse*]. 40. *Ye will not come to me, that ye might have* [eternal] *life*. You search the Scriptures, you [say you] believe the Prophets, which you cannot but see testify of me, and yet you will not *come to me* [i.e., to God's messiah], to whom they [i.e., the Prophets] direct you."

It would be exceptionally remarkable to see a traditional, eighteenth-century Christian like Jennens commending post-Jesus Jews for paying praiseworthy respect to the Prophets. The books of the prophets (for example, Haggai, Hosea, Isaiah, Jeremiah, Malachi, Nahum, and Zechariah) figure heavily in Jennens's scripture collection for *Messiah*. The very existence of Jennens's resolutely typological, prophecy-and-fulfillment libretto would, I should think, speak powerfully against any notion of his according Jews respect for their admirable veneration of the Prophets.

In my estimation, concluding that Jennens's response *reverses* Holdsworth's pejorative use of the word *Jew* is radically unwarranted, both textually and contextually. If there's one thing traditional Christians like Jennens would hold about the respect Jews pay to the Prophets, it's that their veneration is fundamentally—

indeed damningly—inadequate; that is, according to this view, if Jews truly respected biblical prophecy, they would have become *Christians*.

CONCLUSION

I've several times been told that I am remiss in not providing, when all is said and done, some level of comfort to those Christians who are understandably distressed by what has been brought to light about this beloved, Christian-faith-inspiring oratorio, a work whose glory they had long enjoyed as untainted. I considered it better not to accommodate these distressed *Messiah* lovers, however, principally because I was concerned that to agree that Christian discomfort ought to be assuaged here could, in a certain way, appear to be giving in to the Christian triumphalism I aim to resist: I thought it would too readily appear to be yielding to the notion that spiritual solace, particularly *Christian* solace, is the end game of all religious scrutiny. The harsh truth is that the long history of Christianity also involves a long history of anti-Judaic (and other) contempt. I saw Handel's *Messiah* very much within this anti-Judaic history, and so I took the oratorio to be, in at least some significant part, a regrettably uncomfortable work.

I've also been told by others that my work on Handel's *Messiah* trivializes the Holocaust, because I (implicitly) equate or link the mass murder of Jews in World War II with what they consider my fantasized rejoicing against Judaism within what is surely a harmless piece of beautiful art music.

Here I cannot emphasize strongly enough what I said earlier in this essay: the present book is not about exterminationist, so-called racial antisemitism but rather about exulting at the (believed) everlasting divine condemnation of the religion of Judaism and its practitioners. For the purposes of this inquiry I chose to act as though I were agnostic on whether disdain for Judaism can or must lead to the "racial" antisemitism of the Third Reich. I took Christian rejoicing against Judaism to be a troubling and attention-worthy phenomenon in and of itself.

And as for the validity of my notion of *Messiah*'s anti-Judaic schadenfreude in the first place: from studying the biblical and historical contexts, I would judge that hearing Handel's *Messiah* as an example of rejoicing against Judaism is closer to "reporting the news" than to fantasy.

So with Old Israel supposedly rejected by God and its obsolescence long ago secured by the ostensibly permanent destruction of the Temple, why would an eighteenth-century text and musical setting rejoice against Judaism whatsoever, whether explicitly or, as in *Messiah*, implicitly? There must have been some festering Christian anxiety about the prolonged survival of Judaism. How can a "false" religion last so long? Might Judaism somehow actually be "true"?

Judaism was experienced as theologically (not socially) rather threatening to many Christians of Jennens's and Handel's day.[41] These Jewish questions were, indeed, a matter of eternal life and death, says one of Jennens's key guides, the *Messiah* source we began with, Bishop Kidder's *Demonstration of the Messias, . . . Especially against the Jews*: "If we [Christians] be wrong in . . . [theological] dispute with the Jews, we err fundamentally, and must never hope for salvation [from an eternity in hell]. So that either we or the Jews must be in a state of damnation. Of such great importance are those matters in dispute between us and them." This would represent ample motivation for the text and musical setting of *Messiah* to engage these issues and would perhaps help explain any lapse from decent Christian gratitude into unseemly rejoicing in the Hallelujah chorus.

While still a timely, living masterpiece that may rightly continue to bring great spiritual and aesthetic sustenance to many of us music lovers, Christian or otherwise, *Messiah* also appears to be very much a work of its own era. Listeners might do well to ponder exactly what it means when, in keeping with centuries-long tradition (whatever the origin or cause of this tradition),[42] they *stand* during concert performances of the Hallelujah chorus.

III

THE *MESSIAH* LIBRETTO

This part of the book is meant primarily as a general reference work but also as an additional means to further contextualize and support the primary arguments of the main essay, in chapter 2. Both the essay and the annotated libretto, however, are designed in a way that they can be profitably be read in isolation.

The annotated libretto primarily focuses on providing biblical background. In Jennens's and Handel's day, authors and composers could (and did) rely on their audience to understand the contexts of a biblical libretto—essentially the King James Version of the Bible (KJV) and the *Book of Common Prayer* (BCP). Most middle- and upper-class homes had easy access to both these sources, but with the founding of the Society for Promoting Christian Knowledge (SPCK) in 1698, inexpensive editions of both the KJV and BCP meant that lower-middle-class and even working-class homes could afford to own both. By the time *Messiah* performances became popular, generations of ordinary English people had access to these sources. Furthermore, commentaries on both the Bible and the BCP were found in the libraries of the middle class and especially of the clergy. Even the illiterate or partially literate imbibed the substance of these commentaries, since they were the quarries that the clergy dug into for the sermons they preached from their pulpits—both conformist (Anglican) and nonconformist (non-Anglican). Finally, it's worth noting that a large part of religious education in the schools was learning by rote extended passages from Scripture and the BCP.

So those who heard *Messiah* for the first time and subsequently during the later eighteenth century would have readily understood the theological and religious contexts within which *Messiah* was written—and fairly readily recognized the sources that were being quoted, including the phrases and sentences that were omitted. But that is not the case today. People who hear *Messiah* today—even many strongly religious people—do not have this kind of biblical knowledge to draw upon, and therefore do not appreciate the nuanced meanings and understandings that are implicit (and explicit, in their sequence) in Jennens's libretto.

A WORD ON MESSIANIC EXPECTATIONS IN TRADITIONAL CHRISTIANITY AND JUDAISM

Jennens's *Messiah* libretto assumes a basic knowledge of traditional Christian understandings of the term *messiah*. Because most listeners, including many observant Christians, today don't have this knowledge, and because the quasi-narrative flow of Jennens's libretto barely makes sense without it, I will attempt a brief survey of certain aspects in the traditional Christian understandings of the messiah concept. I'll also highlight some of its differences from certain aspects of traditional Jewish understandings. In this I have relied heavily on Donald Juel's marvelous book, *Messianic Exegesis: Christological Interpretation of the Old Testament in Early Christianity* (1988).

In the canonical Hebrew biblical texts, a *mashiyach* ("anointed one") is an agent of God who is anointed, with oil, into the service of God's covenant people Israel. The designation was used especially for the kings of Israel, like Saul, David, Solomon, and Zedekiah. Sometimes it was also used for priests or prophets.

The dynasty of the kings of Israel was named after its greatest "anointed one," King David. After the Davidic dynasty was defeated many centuries before the time of Jesus, Israel's prophetic writers promised a future "David" who would bring a restoration of the monarchy, although it should perhaps be noted that they did not refer to this future David specifically with the title of *mashiyach* (see, for example, Jeremiah 30:9 and Ezekiel 37:24). This restoration would be a time when foreigners no longer ruled over Israel, and when they (that is, the foreigners, "the gentiles"), together with Israel, would serve the one true God and God's great Davidic king. The biblical book of Daniel, at 9:25–26, refers to a coming (Davidic?) "anointed leader" and to an "anointed one," both of whom Christians traditionally understand to be the Anointed One: God's messiah, Jesus.[1]

The Hebrew word *mashiyach* was rendered with the word *christos* in the Septuagint, the hallowed Greek translation of the Hebrew biblical texts begun in Egypt a few centuries before the time of Jesus. The Septuagint's variant readings, rather than the demonstrably or presumably original Hebrew readings, were often the ones that were quoted in the (Greek) books that came to form the New Testament.

Thus, for example, Matthew 1:22–23 reads: "Now all this [namely, the way that the birth of Jesus of Nazareth took place] was done, that it might be fulfilled which was spoken of the Lord by the prophet [at Isaiah 7:14], saying, Behold, a virgin shall be with child, and shall bring forth a son, and they shall call his name Emmanuel, which being interpreted [from the Hebrew, *imanu El*] is, 'God with us.'" The rendering *virgin* comes not, strictly, from the

Hebrew text of Isaiah 7:14, which reads "Hiney ha'*almah* harah veyoledet ben veqarat shemo 'imanu'el" ("Look, the *young woman* is with child and about to give birth to a son, and she will call him Immanuel"), but from the Greek Septuagint, which here speaks of "the *parthenos*" (possibly "the *young woman*," but most likely "the *virgin*," which is the sense clearly conveyed when this passage is quoted in the Gospel of Matthew).

In the New Testament, Jesus of Nazareth is given the name Iesous Christos, or Jesus Christ (that is, "Jesus Messiah"), and he is confessed to be God's promised *mashiyach* (which, as mentioned, was rendered with the word *christos* in the Septuagint), as for example when he is given this title in Acts 2:36, which reads: "Therefore let all the house of Israel know assuredly, that God hath made that same Jesus, whom ye have crucified, both Lord and Christ."

The concept of the "*crucified* Messiah" does create challenges for those who recognize that the canonical Hebrew biblical texts don't appear clearly or explicitly to talk of a coming Davidic leader or *mashiyach* who suffers an ignoble death, much less of a *mashiyach* who atones for human sin, as is proclaimed, for example, in the New Testament at 1 Corinthians 15:3: "For I [the apostle Paul] delivered unto you [followers of Jesus] first of all, that [good news] which I also received, how [it is the case] that [Jesus] *Christ* died [sacrificially, on the cross] for our sins according to the [ancient] Scriptures [of Israel]."

The traditional Christian belief that Jesus is "*the* Messiah" who suffers and atones by dying on a cross—or, at least, that *Jesus* was God's messiah—has of course for centuries played the central role in traditional Christianity's vigorous disagreements with traditional Judaism. This role is apparent already in the apostles' missionary preaching in Acts 1–4, the New Testament material that figures so heavily, as we saw, in part 2 of Jennens's *Messiah* libretto.

Jews who believe in a coming Davidic messiah customarily see in the canonical Hebrew biblical texts that God has given them good reason to expect a *mashiyach* who literally restores Israel and ushers in a messianic age of literal peace, but they have customarily seen no clear reason to expect a Davidic messiah who rules only spiritually, who brings only spiritual peace, who is in any sense God himself (and who is therefore to be *worshipped*), and who suffers and atones for sin by dying on a cross (that is to say, they do *not* expect a messiah who behaves in the set of ways that Jesus of Nazareth is depicted in the New Testament).[2]

Christians, however, experience in Jesus the one true God revealed to Israel. They customarily proclaim the New Testament's "good news" that God's promised kingdom has been realized in God's messiah, Jesus. By his sacrificial death Jesus redeems humanity from sin, and he rules the cosmos as God the Son, in a holy Trinity or "tri-unity" with "God the Father" and "God the Holy Spirit."

Christians have customarily read the passages from the canonical Hebrew biblical texts that speak of a suffering figure—one who is "brought as a lamb to the slaughter," who is "despised and rejected of men," who is "a man of sorrows and acquainted with grief," who gives "his back to the smiters," who is "wounded for our transgressions," and the like—as predictions of what would happen to Jesus. Though as a rule unaware of the fact that none of these so-called suffering-servant passages speaks of him explicitly as an "anointed one" (that is, as a *mashiyach*), traditional Christians would say that, by simple virtue of Christ Jesus' suffering, these predictions of a suffering servant have to be categorized as "messianic."[3]

Jews, however, have customarily read these passages as referring not to a single coming figure but to God's servant the people Israel (see, for example, Isaiah 41:8–9), delivered from exile.

If Jesus is the God of Israel's promised Messiah, as Christians proclaim, then at least from the perspective of a disinterested reading of the Hebrew biblical texts held sacred by both Christians and Jews, God might appear to have had a change of mind about what the Davidic leader or messiah would be like: from an immediately triumphant, now literally ruling Anointed One who immediately prospers to an ultimately triumphant, now spiritually ruling Anointed One who immediately suffers. And so Jews can hardly be blamed—though, until recent times, by Christians they characteristically have been—for not customarily seeing the suffering-servant poetry of Isaiah as (implicitly) *messianic*.

In contrast, Christians cannot be blamed, as they continually have been by Jews, for reading Isaiah messianically in light of what happened to Jesus. As explained in Juel, *Messianic Exegesis*, the New Testament writers, already believing the crucified Jesus to have been God's messiah, will have been reasonably led to draw on Isaiah's suffering-servant poems as potentially messianic texts, since for example the "anointed one" is called the Lord's "servant" at Psalm 89:38–39, just as the "branch" is called the Lord's "servant" at Zechariah 3:8 ("branch" is a designation for the future Davidic king, as seen at Jeremiah 23:5 and 33:15).[4]

God's peaceable kingdom is said in traditional Christian theology to be "proleptic," which means that the messiah Jesus' full rulership, and the peace he brings, is anticipated by his followers in a manner that regards the future event as certain to come and yet, in some sense, already here. Followers of Jesus are able to profess that they live in the biblically promised kingdom of God, even though the world is plainly not yet literally at peace—for that, they await the Second Coming of Christ. The Aramaic formula *maranatha*, found at 1 Corinthians 16:22, neatly captures this future, past, and present: the term can mean "Lord, come" (a prayer for

Christ's Second Coming), or "Our Lord has come" (a confession of Christ's first coming), or "Our Lord is come" (an acknowledgment of Christ's presence in worship).

Thus is Jesus hailed the *mashiyach*, the *christos*; and because he is so acclaimed, his followers are called Christians.

HOW THIS ANNOTATED LIBRETTO IS DESIGNED

This part of the book, then, fully identifies for the first time the historical sources of the libretto from Handel's *Messiah* and offers brief, historically informed commentaries on the texts of each of its movements.

Beginning in part 1 of the oratorio, below the centered headings of Handel's musical numbers, the words are given as found in the compilation of biblical excerpts presented to Handel by his librettist, Charles Jennens. These scriptural passages were originally printed in a "wordbook," something that Handel's audiences could study beforehand and follow along with at performances. I've closely reproduced the readings, orthography, and typeface choices (roman, italic, and all caps) of the wordbook that was printed for the 1743 performances of *Messiah* in London, as this printing is thought to have Jennens's authority. The wordbooks are set off with horizontal lines; the first example is "MAJORA CANAMUS." Occasional, slight differences in the wordings as found in Handel's musical setting are enclosed in brackets and labeled "Handel's setting." Many of these differences seem to derive from the German of the Luther Bible, which suggests that Handel's biblical knowledge was rather close. Consider, for example, movement no. 20, where Jennens, like the KJV of Matthew 11:29b, gives "lowly *in* heart," whereas Handel's setting gives "lowly *of* heart"; the Luther Bible here reads "von Herzen demütig"—"lowly of heart."

Next, where appropriate, are provided my heavily paraphrased renderings of the libretto's biblical selections into modern American English—labeled "Paraphrase" for clarity—as even the "plain-sense" meanings of these KJV and BCP passages are far from obvious to most readers today. Then are provided various notes and explanations based on traditional Christian understandings that were widely taught in sermons and biblical commentaries of Handel's day and that are often similarly taught today among certain Christians, especially in the United States. My aim is to provide insight into the mainstream Protestant Christianity of Jennens's and Handel's time, a Christianity that has much in common with the beliefs of many traditional Christians today. As mentioned in the introduction, I do know, however, that there was in the eighteenth and is in the twenty-first century no monolithic "traditional Christianity."

To show clearly and conveniently the prophetical or typological relationships originally assumed all through *Messiah*, I've provided the full texts of the biblical sources for Jennens's libretto and placed after them their typologically parallel passages from the Old Testament (OT) or New Testament (NT).

Further, I've also indicated within the set-off material the precise prophetical or typological relationships of these biblical excerpts in concise summary. Here are examples of how this works:

- at movement no. 3, the entry "Isaiah 40:4 → Luke 3:5" means that Jennens chose Isaiah 40:4 for Handel to set to music, and that this OT text is quoted in the NT at Luke 3:5

- at movement no. 2, the entry "Isaiah 40:1–3 → Matthew 3:3b / Mark 1:3 / Luke 3:4b, John 1:23" means that Jennens chose Isaiah 40:1–3 for Handel to set to music, and that this OT text is quoted in the NT at John 1:23 in one way and at Matthew 3:3b, Mark 1:3, and Luke 3:4b in a second way

- at movement no. 19, the entry "Isaiah 35:5–6 → Matthew 11:5, Mark 7:37, Luke 7:22" means that Jennens chose Isaiah 35:5–6 for Handel to set to music, and that this OT text is quoted at Matthew 11:5 in one way, at Mark 7:37 in a second way, and at Luke 7:22 in a third way

- at movement no. 8, the entry "Isaiah 7:14 ↔ Matthew 1:22–23" means that OT Isaiah 7:14 is quoted at NT Matthew 1:22–23, and that Jennens compiled his wording from both of these biblical passages

- at movement no. 20, "Matthew 11:28–29 ← Jeremiah 6:16" means that Jennens chose Matthew 11:28–29 for Handel to set to music, and that this NT text quotes from the OT at Jeremiah 6:16

- at movement no. 6, the brackets at "Malachi 3:2 → [Revelation 6:16–17]" signify that the OT text Malachi 3:2 is strongly alluded to but not actually quoted in the NT text Revelation 6:16–17

- if only an OT text is indicated (as, e.g., at movement no. 30) or only a NT text is indicated (as, e.g., at movement no. 14b), this means that the text Jennens gave to Handel is not quoted in the other Testament.

All biblical source quotations, unless otherwise noted, are from eighteenth-century editions of the KJV and BCP. Having to distinguish between readings of this Bible and this prayer book comes up mostly for passages from the Psalms.

Boldface in the biblical quotations indicates wording that Jennens has skipped over within a verse, and underlining signals textual emendations to the KJV and BCP that Jennens has adopted. Jennens's emendation sources, mostly from seventeenth- and eighteenth-century reference works, are provided at the end of each number. (Full bibliographical entries for those titles are found in the Works Cited at the end of the book.)

MESSIAH, an ORATORIO.

Set to Musick by George-Frideric Handel, Esq;.

MAJORA CANAMUS.

Virgil, Eclogue IV
***Sicelides Musae, paulo** majora canamus* . . .

trans. Trapp 1731
"[Let us] raise a loftier strain . . ."

And without Controversy, great is the Mystery of Godliness: God was
manifested in the Flesh, justify'd by the Spirit, seen of Angels, preached
among the Gentiles, *believed on in the World, received up in Glory.*

Notes:

1. Pairs being brought together in this rendering of the NT hymn involve flesh and spirit and humans and angels, such that Jews, however, are
absent from this (KJV-based) picture.

2. Jennens was probably aware from the remarkably detailed arguments
in the biblical commentaries he owned that the then-standard reading
"God" in 1 Timothy 3:16 was controversial. Some ancient Greek NT manuscripts (the best ones, it turns out) read "who" at this spot, not "God,"
making the passage speak not of God made manifest in the flesh as Jesus
Christ, but theologically more unexceptionally of "the mystery of godliness" made manifest. The alteration from *who* to *God* probably occurred

in the third century; this easily happened, or was facilitated, no doubt because the abbreviation for *God* in Greek (theta-sigma) looks much like the word for *who* (an omicron and a sigma).

NT 1 Timothy 3:16
And without controversy, great is the mystery of godliness: God was <u>manifest</u> in the flesh, justified <u>in</u> the Spirit, seen of angels, preached <u>unto</u> the Gentiles, believed on in the world, received up <u>into</u> glory.

Hammond 1653, 1 Timothy 3:16
And without controversy great is the mystery of godliness, God was <u>manifest</u> in (*margin*, "manifested <u>by</u>") the flesh, justified <u>in</u> (*margin*, "by") the spirit, seen of Angels, preached <u>unto</u> (*margin*, "among") the Gentiles, believed on in the world, received up <u>into</u> (*margin*, "in," or "<u>with</u>") glory.

In whom are hid all the Treasures of Wisdom and Knowledge.

NT Colossians 2:3
In whom are hid all the treasures of wisdom and knowledge.

Note:

The KJV of Colossians 2:2b–3 reads, "to acknowledgment of the mystery of God, and of the Father, and of [Jesus] Christ; in whom [*KJV margin:* "*or*, wherein"] are hid all the treasures of wisdom and knowledge." At 2:3, the reading "in whom" would refer to the antecedent word *Christ*. The reading "wherein," however, would refer to the word *mystery*.

MESSIAH, AN ORATORIO

PART ONE

[1] Sinfony

I.

[2] Recit accomp

Comfort ye, comfort ye my People, saith your God; speak ye comfortably
to *Jerusalem*, and cry unto her, that her Warfare is accomplished, that
her Iniquity is pardon'd.

The Voice of him that crieth in the Wilderness, Prepare ye the Way of the
Lord, make straight in the Desert a Highway for our God.

Isaiah 40:1–3 → Matthew 3:3b / Mark 1:3 / Luke 3:4b, John 1:23

Paraphrase

*"Give comfort to them, you prophets, give comfort to my people
[who expect my messiah, Jesus]," says your God. "You prophets
must speak words of comfort to Jerusalem, and you must shout out
to them that their strife is over, and that their sin is forgiven." The
prophetic, comforting voice of John the Baptist shouts out, in the
wilderness, "Make ready the way of the Lord; make a straight path
in the desert for our God: the Son, Jesus, God's messiah."*

Notes:

1. The unspecified *ye* of OT Isaiah 40:1 is typically understood as "you *prophets*." In the Septuagint (the pre-Christian translation of the Hebrew biblical texts into Greek, an important source for writers of the NT), however, the *ye* are identified as priests; there Isaiah 40:2 reads, "O *priests*, speak to the heart of Jerusalem; comfort her."

2. "Jerusalem" and "my people" here at OT Isaiah 40 are typically taken by traditional Christian readers to mean God's faithful, messiah-expecting, covenant people of Israel, that is, the (proto–)Christian Church.

3. Often in traditional Christian understandings, this "strife" was taken to mean the time of affliction under the Law of Moses, under Old Israel, the synagogue, Judaism. The strife of God's people is over because they accept the gospel of Jesus, God the Son, God's messiah, the deliverer of the long-promised new covenant with God's people, New Israel, the church, Christianity. (In Judaism, however, the traditional reception of this text has been quite different. With the book of Isaiah's main message being one of comfort and reconciliation, several portions of chapters 40 and following are recited, as they were in Handel's day, in the synagogue for the haftarah, or prophetic readings, on the sabbaths following Tishah B'Av, a day of public mourning and fasting that commemorates the destructions of the Temple in 586 BCE and 70 CE.)

4. John the Baptist is the "spirit of Elijah" (NT Luke 1:17) who announces the coming of God's messiah. Elijah was predicted, at OT Malachi 4:5, to appear before the coming of God's messiah, the "day of the Lord."

5. The "desert" was, in traditional Christian understandings, often read in two ways simultaneously: (1) generally and metaphorically as the sinful state of the world and (2) specifically and literally as Judea, the place where Jesus, God's messiah, makes his appearance, the desert or wilderness also being the place in which John the Baptist conducted his messiah-preparing ministry.

6. Regarding a Christian understanding of "Jerusalem," see NT Galatians 4:22–26, as quoted here (several paragraphs below, right before the heading for the next movement in the libretto).

OT Isaiah 40:1–3

Comfort ye, comfort ye my people, saith your God. Speak ye comfortably to Jerusalem, and cry unto her, that her warfare is accomplished, that her iniquity is pardoned: **for she hath received of the Lord's hand double for all her sins**. The voice of him that crieth in the wilderness, Prepare ye the way of the Lord, make straight in the desert a high-way for our God.

NT Matthew 3:3b / Mark 1:3 / Luke 3:4b

The voice of one [i.e., the voice of John, the Baptist—Matthew 3:1, Mark 1:4, Luke 3:2] crying in the wilderness, Prepare ye the way of the Lord, make his paths straight.

NT John 1:23

The voice of one crying in the wilderness [i.e., the voice of John the Baptist—John 1:19], Make straight the way of the Lord, as said the prophet Esias.

(See also NT Galatians 4:22–26

It is written [i.e., at OT Genesis 16 and 21], that Abraham had two sons, the one by a bondmaid [i.e., the slave Hagar, mother of Ishmael], the other by a freewoman [i.e., Sarah, the mother of Isaac]. . . . Which things are an allegory: for these are the two covenants (*KJV marginal note:* "*Or*, testaments"); the one from the mount Sinai [i.e., where the Law of Moses was given—signifying *Old Israel*, Judaism], which gendereth to bondage, . . . But Jerusalem which is above is free [i.e., not the earthly "Jerusalem which now is," but the heavenly "Jerusalem which is above"—signifying *New Israel*, Christianity].)

[3] Song

Every Valley shall be exalted, and every Mountain and Hill made low, the Crooked straight, and the rough Places plain.

Isaiah 40:4 → Luke 3:5

Paraphrase

[Says God, further:] "With the coming of God's messiah, Jesus, every valley will be filled in, and every mountain and hill will be leveled; the crooked places will be made straight, and the rough places will be made smooth."

Note:

These violent predictions were in Christianity traditionally considered a good thing, a series of metaphors: with the coming of the gospel, the lowly will be raised up and the high and mighty brought down; and the crooked ways of sinful humanity will be made straight.

OT Isaiah 40:4
Every valley shall be exalted, and every mountain and hill **shall be** made low: **and** the crooked **shall be made** straight, and the rough places plain:

NT Luke 3:5
Every valley shall be filled, and every mountain and hill shall be brought low; and the crooked shall be made straight, and the rough ways shall be made smooth.

[4] Chorus

And the Glory of the Lord shall be revealed, and all Flesh shall see it together; for the Mouth of the Lord hath spoken it.

Isaiah 40:5 → Luke 3:6

Paraphrase

[Says God, further:] "And in God's messiah, Jesus, the saving glory of the Lord God will be revealed; and everybody, together, will see

God's glory, in Jesus; for the Lord God, through the prophet, has said so."

OT Isaiah 40:5
And the glory of the LORD shall be revealed, and all flesh shall see it together: for the mouth of the LORD hath spoken it.

NT Luke 3:6
And all flesh shall see the salvation of God.

(See also NT Hebrews 1:1–3
God . . . hath in these last days spoken unto us by his Son [i.e., Jesus], . . . who is the brightness of his [i.e., God's] glory, and the express image of his person.)

II.

[5] Recit accomp

Thus saith the Lord of Hosts: Yet once a little while, and I will shake the
    Heavens and the Earth; the Sea, and the dry Land:
And I will shake all Nations; and the Desire of all Nations shall come.

Haggai 2:6–7 → Hebrews 12:25–26

Paraphrase

This is what the Lord God of Heavenly Armies says: "Wait yet a little while longer, and once more I am going to shake the sky and the earth, the sea, and the dry land: and I am going to shake up all nations; and the desire of all nations [—my messiah—] will come."

Notes:

1. This part of the book of Haggai, in earlier historical context, concerns a divine announcement that a new Temple, after the destruction of the older Temple in 586 BCE, will indeed be an appropriate Temple for the Lord.

2. The "Lord of Hosts" is the Lord God of the armies of angels surrounding God's throne (e.g., OT 1 Samuel 4:4).

3. The previous time that the Lord God shook the sky and earth was when God, through Moses, gave the Law to Israel at Mount Sinai. God will shake the earth and sky again when, through Jesus, God gives the new covenant to God's people: New Israel, the believers in God's messiah, Jesus.

4. What the KJV renders as "the desire of all nations" has in Christianity traditionally been understood to mean God's messiah.

OT Haggai 2:6–7

For thus saith the LORD of hosts; Yet once, **it is** a little while, and
I will shake the heavens, and the earth, **and** the sea, and the dry
land: And I will shake all nations, and the desire of all nations shall
come: **and I will fill this house with glory, saith the** LORD **of hosts.**

NT Hebrews 12:25–26

See that ye [i.e., you followers of "Jesus the author and finisher of
our faith"—Hebrews 12:2] refuse not him [i.e., God] that speaketh:
For if they [i.e., the ancient Israelites] escaped not who refused him
that spake on earth [i.e., God (or Moses?), at Mount Sinai], much
more shall not we [i.e., the followers of Jesus] escape, if we turn
away from him [i.e., God] that speaketh from heaven: Whose voice
then [i.e., at the giving of the Law of Moses to Israel at Sinai—OT
Exodus 19:18] shook the earth: but now [i.e., at the advent of
God's messiah] he [i.e., God] hath promised, saying, Yet once more
I shake not the earth only, but also heaven.

[5] Recit accomp, *continued*

The Lord whom ye seek shall suddenly come to his Temple, even the Messenger of the Covenant, whom ye delight in: Behold He shall come, saith the Lord of Hosts.

Malachi 3:1 → [Matthew 3:3; 11:10; Mark 1:2–3; Luke 1:76, 7:27]

Paraphrase

"[Look, once my messenger, John the Baptist, has prepared the way,] the Lord that you are expecting—God's messiah—will come suddenly to God's Temple at Jerusalem, namely the Messenger of the (New) Covenant, Jesus, the one you will take delight in: Look, he is going to come," says the Lord of Heavenly Armies.

OT Malachi 3:1
Behold, I will send my messenger, and he shall prepare the way before me: and the Lord whom ye seek, shall suddenly come to his temple: even the messenger of the covenant, whom ye delight in: behold, he shall come, saith the LORD of hosts.

(See NT Matthew 3:3; 11:10; Mark 1:2–3; Luke 1:76, 7:27 for parallels to OT Malachi 3:1a.)

[6] Song (*or* Recit?)[5]

But who may abide the Day of his coming? And who shall stand when He appeareth?
For He is like a Refiner's Fire:

Malachi 3:2 → [Revelation 6:16–17]

Paraphrase

But who will be able to endure the day of wrath when God's messiah comes? And who will be able to stand and face him when he appears? For in his wrath God's messiah is like the white heat of a fire for refining silver and gold.

OT Malachi 3:2

But who may abide the day of his coming? and who shall stand when he appeareth? for he is like a refiner's fire, **and like fullers'** [i.e., launderers'] **soap.**

(See also NT Revelation 6:16–17

Hide us [i.e., various men, high and lowly—Revelation 6:15] from . . . the wrath of the Lamb [i.e., Jesus, the "Lamb of God"]: For the great day of his wrath is come; and who shall be able to stand?)

[7] Chorus

And He shall purify the Sons of Levi, *that they may offer unto the Lord an Offering in Righteousness.*

Malachi 3:3 → Hebrews 7:5,11–12

Paraphrase

And God's messiah will purify the Levites, [the imperfect priesthood of the Jerusalem Temple, of their ritual perversions and abuses,] so that they, [transformed as a holy priesthood of New Israel, the church,] may righteously give to the Lord God a proper [spiritual] offering.

Notes:

1. Purifying the sons of Levi was taken in many traditional Christian interpretations, especially before World War II, to point to the year 70 CE, when Roman soldiers destroyed the Jerusalem Temple. According to this belief, Jesus—seated in heaven at the right hand of God, forty years after his having been crucified—vented his anger, via the Roman armies, at Jewish failure to accept him as messiah.

2. A prevalent traditional Christian understanding is that Old Israel's Temple priesthood worshiped God carnally by offering material sacrifices and teaching the Law of Moses, whereas the purified priesthood of God is active in a new, converted, spiritual "true Israel"—the Christian Church—which worships God properly: through and in Jesus, God the Son. Thus, Jewish worship, centered on the Law of Moses, is rendered obsolete, to be entirely superseded by Christian worship, centered on the gospel of Jesus.

OT Malachi 3:3
And he shall **sit as a refiner and purifier of silver: and he shall** purify the sons of Levi, **and purge them as gold and silver**, that they may offer unto the LORD an offering in righteousness.

NT Hebrews 7:5,11–12
The sons of Levi[:] . . . If therefore perfection were by the Levitical priesthood (for under it the people [i.e., Old Israel, "the Jews"] received the law [i.e., the Law of Moses]), what further need was there that another priest [i.e., God's messiah, Jesus] should rise after the order of Melchisedec [i.e., the ancient king of Jerusalem and priest of the most high God—who prefigures God's messiah Jesus as king and priest], and not be called after the order of Aaron [i.e., the brother of Moses, and ancestor of the Levitical priesthood]? For the priesthood being changed [i.e., from the order of Aaron to the order of Melchisedec, namely from the Jewish Temple to the Christian Church], there is made of necessity a change also of the law.

(See also NT 1 Peter 2:5

Ye [i.e., you followers of Jesus] . . . are built up a spiritual house, an
holy priesthood to offer up spiritual sacrifices, acceptable to God by
Jesus Christ.)

(See also NT John 4:19–24.)

III.
[8] Recit

Behold, a Virgin shall conceive, and bear a Son, and shall call his name
Emmanuel, GOD WITH Us.

Isaiah 7:14 ↔ Matthew 1:22–23

Paraphrase

*Look, a virgin, Mary of Nazareth, will be with child, [miraculously,
by God the Holy Spirit,] and [—while remaining a virgin—] give
birth to a son, Jesus, God's messiah; and even as his name will be
"Jesus," he will be given the designation "Emmanuel," which means
"WITH-US-IS-GOD"; [that is to say: in Jesus, God is with us who are
Jesus' followers—"always, even until the End of the world" (Matthew 28:20)].*

Notes:

1. Traditional Christian interpretations have often asserted that the Hebrew word *alma* at OT Isaiah 7:14 properly signifies a virgin and have
frequently claimed that in the Hebrew biblical texts *alma* is consistently
used in this sense. But when, for example, OT Proverbs 30:19 expresses
wonder at "the way of a man with *an alma*," the author is presumably just

marveling at, or surprised at, the way of a man with a young woman, not with a (young—or old!) virgin in particular. (Note that considering the parallelisms in the Hebrew text of Proverbs 30:18–19, the better translation would be "the way of a man *in* [or, *into*] an alma"; and, strictly speaking at least, as soon as a man is in an *alma*, she is not a virgin.)

2. In depicting Mary of Nazareth as a virgin, the author of the Gospel of Matthew is drawing not on the Hebrew text of Isaiah 7:14, but on the Septuagint, the pre-Christian translation of the Hebrew biblical texts into Greek. In the Septuagint the word *parthenos* does most likely refer to a woman who is a virgin. (On purely lexical grounds, however, the *parthenos* of Isaiah 7:14 could well simply refer to a woman who was virginal up to the moment of conception, that is, not to a woman who gives birth without her egg having been fertilized by a human spermatozoon; consider also the Septuagint of Genesis 34:3, where Dinah, the daughter of Jacob and Leah, after she was "abased" by Schechem, son of Hamor the Hivite, is called "the parthenos," that is, she is to be understood as "the raped virgin.")

Jews and Christians have vigorously disagreed for many centuries on how to understand the woman of Isaiah 7:14. Many Christians up to and including in Handel's day (and beyond, to the present) even suggested that Jews invented the now standard Hebrew wording of Isaiah to confound Christians, such that the earlier, now-lost Hebrew wording would unambiguously have referred to a "virgin"; in this view, the Septuagint reading and NT usage would more accurately reflect the earliest Hebrew text of Isaiah.

But seeing that the Dead Sea Scrolls give *alma* at 7:14 in their text of Isaiah (which was produced at least a century before the birth of Jesus and unearthed only in the twentieth century), the pre-Christian Hebrew wording of Isaiah will doubtless have read not "virgin" but "young woman" all along.

It may be worth noting that, so far as anyone knows, no pre- or non-Christian Jewish texts saw Isaiah 7:14 as predicting the birth of God's messiah.

3. "God-with-us" enframes the Gospel of Matthew, at 1:23 and 28:20 (see also 18:20).

OT Isaiah 7:14

Therefore the Lord himself shall give you a sign, Behold, a virgin shall conceive, and bear a son, and shall call his name <u>Immanuel.</u>

Wells, Isaiah 7:14
Behold, a virgin shall conceive, and bear a son, and shall call his name Emmanuel.

Hebrew Text, Isaiah 7:14
... *ha'alma* ... ("the young woman")

Greek Septuagint, Isaiah 7:14
... *parthenos* ... (most likely, "virgin"; or possibly, "young woman")

NT Matthew 1:22–23
Now all this [i.e., the way that the birth of Jesus Christ took place—Matthew 1:18] was done, that it might be fulfilled which was spoken of the Lord by the prophet, saying, Behold, a virgin shall be with child, and shall bring forth a son, and they shall call his name Emmanuel, which being interpreted is, God with us.

(See also NT Matthew 28:20
And, lo, I [i.e., Jesus] am with you [i.e., the disciples of Jesus—Matthew 28:16—and by extension, traditionally, *the church*] alway, even unto the end of the world [i.e., until the Day of Judgment]. Amen.)

Or:

NT Matthew 1:23
Behold, a virgin shall <u>be with child</u>, and **shall** <u>bring forth</u> a son, and **they** shall call his name Emmanuel, **which being interpreted is,** God with us.

OT Isaiah 7:14
Therefore the Lord himself shall give you [i.e., shall give to you, the House of David—Isaiah 7:13] a sign, Behold, a virgin shall conceive, and bear a son, and shall call his name Immanuel.

[9] Song

O thou that tellest good Tidings to Zion, *get thee up into the high Moun-*
tain: O thou that tellest good Tidings to Jerusalem, *lift up thy Voice with*
Strength; lift it up, be not afraid: Say unto the Cities of Judah, *Behold*
your God.

[Handel's setting, extra: *O thou that tellest good Tidings to Zion*]

Isaiah 40:9 → [Hebrews 12:22–24]

Paraphrase

O you who tells the good news of the birth of Jesus, God's messiah;
you who spreads the gospel to Zion: get yourself up on the high
mountain. O you who tells the good news to Jerusalem: raise your
voice, with power. Raise it, don't be afraid. Say to the cities of Israel's
tribe Judah, "Look, your God, Jesus, is here [out of Bethlehem in the
land of Judah (Matthew 2:6)]."

Notes:

1. *Zion* is the name for the place where God dwells—formerly, in the
Jerusalem Temple, on Mount Zion. The name *Zion* was adopted (NT He-
brews 12:22; Revelation 14:1) for the Christian Church, the place where
God dwells now that the Lord God has apparently rejected the Temple.

2. "The high mountain," because that's where one can best be seen and
heard.

3. Jerusalem is "the city of God," the place where God has dwelled, in
the Temple. The name *Jerusalem*, or *New Jerusalem*, or *heavenly Jerusalem* (NT Hebrews 12:22), was therefore adopted for the church, the place
where God dwells now that the Lord God has apparently rejected old
Jerusalem.

4. Judah is the Southern Kingdom, ruled by the line of King David, the line from which the Anointed One—God's messiah—is expected to come. David united Judah with Israel, the Northern Kingdom, and this united kingdom of south and north also was called Israel.

On the death of David's son, King Solomon, Judah and Israel became once again divided kingdoms, and remained so. But the broader concept of the greater Israel lived on, ideally, as "the Chosen People," the worshipers of the God of Abraham, Isaac, and Jacob.

This later Judaism understood itself as heir of God's promises to Abraham and his descendants. Traditional Christianity, however, came to understand itself as sole legitimate heir.

5. Jennens goes with the KJV's alternate version of OT Isaiah 40:9 (reflecting the Greek Septuagint and the Latin Vulgate Bible, whose understandings of this verse were supported by many Protestant commentators), which reads not "O Zion, that bringest good tidings, . . . O Jerusalem, that bringest good tidings" but "O thou that tellest good tidings to Zion . . . O thou that tellest good tidings to Jerusalem." In *Messiah*, Zion and Jerusalem are not supposed to bear the good tidings of the gospel; they are supposed, rather, to receive (and *accept*) them. On Zion and Jerusalem as receivers, see also OT Isaiah 40:1–3 at the libretto's no. 2, above; and Isaiah 52:7 at the libretto's no. 38c/38d, below.

OT Isaiah 40:9

O Zion, that bringest good tidings [*KJV marginal note:* "*Or*, O thou that tellest good tidings to Zion."], get thee up into the high mountain: O Jerusalem, that bringest good tidings [*KJV marginal note:* "*Or*, O thou that tellest good tidings to Jerusalem."], lift up thy voice with strength: lift it up, be not afraid: say unto the cities of Judah, Behold your God.

Wells, Isaiah 40:9

O thou that tellest good tidings to Zion, get thee up into the high mountain: O thou that tellest good tidings to Jerusalem, lift up thy voice with strength: lift it up, be not afraid: say unto the cities of Judah, Behold your God.

(See also NT Hebrews 12:22–24

But ye [i.e., followers of Jesus] are come unto mount Sion [i.e., where the *gospel of Jesus* is given, in contrast to mount Sinai, where the *law of Moses* is given], and unto the city of the living God, the heavenly Jerusalem, . . . to the general assembly and church of the firstborn [i.e., the church of Jesus], . . . the mediator of the new covenant.)

(See also NT John 12:15

Fear not, daughter of Sion: behold, thy King cometh, sitting on an ass's colt.)

(See also NT Hebrews 7:14

For it is evident that our Lord [i.e., Jesus] sprang out of Juda.)

(See also NT Matthew 2:5–6

For thus it is written by the prophet [i.e., OT Micah 5:2], And thou Bethlehem in the land of Juda, art not the least among the princes of Juda; for out of thee shall come a governor [i.e., God's messiah, Jesus], that shall rule [*KJV marginal note:* "*Or*, feed"] my people Israel.)

[9] Song, *continued*

Arise, shine, for thy Light is come, and the Glory of the Lord is risen upon thee.

Isaiah 60:1 → [John 8:12]

Paraphrase

Get up, you Zion, you new Jerusalem; let your face shine with saving truth; for your light—God's messiah, Jesus—has dawned, and the glory of the Lord God is risen, like the sun, upon you.

Note:

In prevalent traditional Christian understandings, the glory of the Lord is risen upon the church, which succeeds the Temple as the place where God dwells.

OT Isaiah 60:1
Arise, shine, for thy light is come, and the glory of the LORD is risen upon thee.

(See also NT John 8:12
Then spake Jesus again unto them [i.e., the Pharisees, the forerunners of modern, rabbinic Judaism], saying, I am the light of the world; he that followeth me shall not walk in darkness, but shall have the light of life. [*KJV margin:* "Chap. 1.5" (i.e., John 1:5, "And the light [i.e., Jesus] shineth in darkness, and the darkness comprehended it not"; see also John 1:11, "He [i.e., the true light, Jesus] came unto his own [i.e., Old Israel, "the Jews"—see OT Exodus 19:5], and his own received him not").])

& Chorus

[Handel's setting:] *O thou that tellest good Tidings to Zion, good Tidings to Jerusalem, arise; say unto the Cities of Judah, behold your God; behold, the Glory of the Lord is risen upon thee.*

Isaiah 40:9 → [Hebrews 12:22–24]
Isaiah 60:1 → [John 8:12]

(OT Isaiah 40:9a, c with Isaiah 60:1a, c).

[10] Recit accomp

For behold, Darkness shall cover the Earth, and gross Darkness the People; but the Lord shall arise upon thee, and his Glory shall be seen upon thee. And the *Gentiles* shall come to thy Light, and Kings to the Brightness of thy Rising.

Isaiah 60:2–3 → Revelation 21:24

Paraphrase

For, look, darkness will cover the earth, and great darkness [—the captivity of sin—] will cover the peoples of the earth [who will need to walk in the light in order to be those who are saved]. But the Lord God's messiah, the Lord Jesus Christ, God the Son, will, like the sun, arise on you—that is, you among Old Israel who turn to Jesus; you of the "new Jerusalem," the church. And his glory will be seen on you. And the gentiles will come to your saving light of faith in Jesus. And kings will come to your bright dawn.

OT Isaiah 60:2–3
For, behold, **the** darkness shall cover the earth, and gross darkness the people: but the LORD shall arise upon thee, and his glory shall be seen upon thee. And the Gentiles shall come to thy light, and kings to the brightness of thy rising.

(See also NT Revelation 21:24
And the nations of them which are saved, shall walk in the light of it [i.e., the city of new Jerusalem, for which the Lamb of God, Jesus, is the "lamp"]: and the kings of the earth do bring their glory and honour into it.)

[11] Song

The People that walked in Darkness have seen a great Light; [Handel's setting: *and*] *they that dwell in the Land of the Shadow of Death, upon them hath the Light shined.*

Isaiah 9:2 → Matthew 4:16, Luke 1:79

Paraphrase

The people, the whole nation of Israel, who had gone about in the world in darkness [—in captivity to sin, without the full light of the gospel—] have now seen a great saving light: God's messiah, Jesus; and on them who dwell in the land of the shadow of death [—on them who live in grave danger, because sin reigns in their dark, until now Messiah-less world—] has the light shined.

Note:

Traditionally Jews and Christians hold that "the light" in this passage refers to an ideal future ruler, the Messiah.

The apparent past tense verbs of this OT text would be in the "prophetic past tense"—that is, predicting future events but using the past tense—because the events are as good as done. (The straight past tense appears, then, in NT Matthew 4:16.)

OT Isaiah 9:2
The people that walked in darkness, have seen a great <u>light: they</u> that dwell in the land of the shadow of death, upon them hath the light shined.

(See also *Luther Bible*, Isaiah 9:2

. . . *ein grosses Licht: und* . . . ["a great light: and"].)

NT Matthew 4:16

The people which sat in darkness, saw great light: and to them
which sat in the region and shadow of death, light is sprung up.

NT Luke 1:79

To give light to them that sit in darkness, and in the shadow of
death, to guide our feet into the way of peace.

[12] Chorus

---

*For unto us a Child is born, unto us a Son is given; and the Government shall
be upon his Shoulder; and his Name shall be called Wonderful, Counsellor, The Mighty God, The Everlasting Father, The Prince of Peace.*

Isaiah 9:6 → [Luke 1:32]

Paraphrase

*Because to us [—who have seen a great light—] a child, Jesus, God's
messiah, is delivered; to us a son of the Most High is given; and the
government of God's people will rest on Jesus' shoulder; and Jesus
will be called: "Wonderful," "Adviser," "The Powerful God," "The
Everlasting Father," "The Prince of Peace."*

Notes:

1. Many English translations of this passage consider a comma between *wonderful* and *counsellor* to be a mistake—the messianic ruler is
to be called not "Wonderful" and also "Counsellor" but simply "wonder-

ful Counsellor." The question comes up because word division, punctuation, and vowels are not indicated in the ancient Hebrew biblical texts. By a crude but clear analogy: if one were to write the series of letters "RHNSDG," reading them from right to left, as in Hebrew, this could be understood, with their vowels, as "eReHWoNSiDoG," which could yield either "God is now here" or "God is nowhere."

2. In traditional English-language Christian translations and understandings of this messianic verse (OT Isaiah 9:6), the royal child is connected to a divine identity: the son will be called "[The] mighty God." By contrast, the Jewish Publication Society translates this passage as follows: "For a child has been born to us, a son has been given us. And authority has settled on his shoulders. He has been named 'The Mighty God is planning grace; the Eternal Father, a peaceable ruler.'" (That is, the child's name is called "Pele-joez-el-gibbor-Abi-ad-sar-shalom.") This is to reflect the fact that ancient semitic names are often composed of whole sentences that describe a god's actions; for example, the name of the eighth-century BCE Babylonian king Mardukaplaiddina—given as "Merodachbaladan" at, for example, OT Isaiah 39:1—would be rendered from Akkadian into English as "the-god-Marduk-has-provided-an-heir"; the prophet Jeremiah's name means "the-LORD-[Yah(weh)]-exalts"; Isaiah's name means "the-LORD-saves"; and so on. Such names are given to a newborn to describe not the child but the god worshiped by the parents. Thus the long name given to the messianic ruler in Isaiah's text "For unto us a child is born" needn't be describing that child (e.g., by suggesting divinity for him).

There is also the related question of how the Hebrew *elgibbor* from OT Isaiah 9:6 should be translated. The KJV and Jennens render it "The mighty God" and "The Mighty God." Another possible translation is "God ['El'] is a Warrior"; but "Powerful Hero" or "Conquering Hero" are just as or more likely, in which case the issue of Isaiah's prophesying of Jesus as God would be altogether precluded from coming up here. (Note, interestingly, that Luther, who otherwise typically reads the Hebrew biblical texts in a radically Christocentric manner, renders *elgibbor* from Isaiah 9:6 simply as *Held* ["hero"], with neither an adjective nor mention of God.)

3. To see the "Son," Jesus, being hailed as "The Everlasting *Father*" may well seem confusing. Christian interpreters of Isaiah have suggested that God's messiah will be called "The Everlasting Father" on account of Jesus' perpetual paternal care for his people. Note too that in Trinitarian theology Jesus, God the Son, is of *one Being* with "God the Father," light from light.

4. Jesus, God's messiah, will be called "The Prince of Peace," because he is the prince of the war-free time that was established when God became human, in God's messiah Jesus. In traditional Christian understandings, Jesus already rules as God's sovereign, peace-effecting messiah, but at present in a spiritual way only. God's peaceable kingdom is said in traditional Christian theology to be "proleptic," which means that Jesus' full rulership, and the peace he brings, is anticipated by his followers in a manner that regards the future event as certain to come and yet, in some sense, already here. Thus, Christians are able to profess that they live in the biblically promised messianic kingdom of God, even though the world is plainly not yet literally at peace.

5. Curiously, the NT doesn't ever call Jesus what the messianic ruler is called in OT Isaiah 9:6.

OT Isaiah 9:6
For unto us a child is born, unto us a son is given, and the government shall be upon his shoulder: and his name shall be called, Wonderful, Counsellor, The mighty God, The everlasting Father, The Prince of Peace.

(See also NT Luke 1:32
He [i.e., Jesus] shall be great, and shall be called the Son of the Highest; and the Lord God shall give unto him the throne of his father David [i.e., of Jesus' ancestral father, King David].)

(See also NT John 3:16
For God so loved the world, that he gave [i.e., sacrificed] his only begotten Son [i.e., there are other "sons of God," but Jesus is the only son who is *begotten* of God], that whosoever believeth in him [i.e., Jesus], should not perish, but have everlasting life.)

(See also NT Luke 2:11

For unto you is born this day, in the city of David, a saviour, which is Christ the Lord.)

(See also OT Isaiah 9:4

For thou [i.e., God] hast broken the yoke of his [i.e., the nation's, Israel's] burden, and the staff of his shoulder, the rod of his oppressor.)

IV.

[13] Pifa

[14a] Recit

There were Shepherds abiding in the Field, keeping Watch over their Flock by Night.

Luke 2:8 ← [Psalm 70:78]

Paraphrase

In the region where Jesus, God's messiah, was born there were shepherds encamped, keeping watch over their flock during the night.

Note:

Jesus, like the great King David (see OT 1 Samuel 16:1,11–13; Psalm 78:70), will be taken from the sheepfolds of Bethlehem, namely "the city of David" (see NT Luke 2:11 at the libretto's no. 15, below), to be anointed as the royal servant of God.

NT Luke 2:8

And there were **in the same country** shepherds abiding in the field, keeping watch over their flock by night.

(See also OT Psalm 70:78

He [i.e., God] chose David also his servant, and took him from the sheepfolds.)

[14b] Recit accomp, *or* Song

And lo, an Angel of the Lord came upon them, and the Glory of the Lord shone round about them, and they were sore afraid.

Luke 2:9

Paraphrase

And see: an angel of the Lord God appeared among the shepherds, and the Lord's glory shone all around them, and they were extremely afraid.

NT Luke 2:9

And, lo, <u>the</u> angel of the Lord came upon them, and the glory of the Lord shone round about them; and they were sore afraid.

[15] Recit

And the Angel said unto them, Fear not; for behold, I bring you good Tidings of great Joy, which shall be to all People:

For unto you is born this Day, in the City of *David*, a Saviour, which is Christ the Lord.

Luke 2:10–11 ← [Isaiah 9:6]

Paraphrase

And the angel of the Lord God said to the shepherds, "Don't be frightened; because, look, I bring you good news of great joy for all people: because to you is born today, in Bethlehem, the City of King David, a [universal, spiritual] savior, namely Jesus Christ, the Lord.

Notes:

1. At "to all people," the Greek text in Luke reads *panti tō laō*—literally, "all *the* people [singular]," most likely meaning "all the people, namely 'historical [Jewish] Israel.'" Many Christian commentators, however, have—just like the translators of the KJV—understood NT Luke 2:10 clearly to be including gentiles.

2. David was the most powerful king of Israel, a favorite of God, from whose lineage (see NT Luke 1:26,32; 2:4) comes Jesus of Nazareth.

3. Jesus' very name—Yeshua in Aramaic, translated as Yesous in NT Greek and as Iesus in Latin—means "Yah [God] is salvation."

4. The word *Christ* renders the NT Greek word *Christos*, "messiah."

NT Luke 2:10–11
And the angel said unto them, Fear not: for behold, I bring you good tidings of great joy, which shall be to all people. For unto you is born this day, in the city of David, a Saviour, which is Christ the Lord.

(See also OT Isaiah 9:6
For unto us a child is born, unto us a son is given . . .)

(See also OT Micah 5:2
But thou, Bethlehem Ephratah [i.e., the city of David], though thou be little among the thousands of Judah, yet out of thee shall he come forth unto me that is to be ruler in Israel; whose goings

forth have been from of old, from everlasting [*KJV marginal note:* "Hebr(ew). the days of eternity"].)

[16] Recit accomp

And suddenly there was with the Angel a Multitude of the heavenly Host, praising God, and saying, [. . .]

Luke 2:13

Paraphrase

And suddenly there was with the angel of the Lord God a plethora of the Heavenly Army of angels, praising God, and saying,

[this biblical passage continues at the next movement, the libretto's no. 17]

NT Luke 2:13
And suddenly there was with the angel a multitude of the heavenly host praising God, and saying,

[17] Chorus

Glory to God in the Highest, and on Earth Peace [Handel's setting: *Peace on Earth*], *Good Will towards Men.*

Luke 2:14

Paraphrase

[this biblical passage continues from the previous movement, the libretto's no. 16]

"Glory be to God in the highest heavens, and peace on earth, and God's good will toward humankind."

NT Luke 2:14
Glory to God in the highest, and <u>on earth peace</u>, good will towards men.

(See also *Luther Bible*, Luke 2:14
. . . *und Friede auf Erden* . . . ["and peace on earth"].)

(See also *Doddridge*, Luke 2:14
Glory to GOD in the highest; and peace on earth . . .)

V.

[18] Song

Rejoice greatly, O Daughter of Sion, *shout, O Daughter of* Jerusalem; *behold thy King cometh unto thee:*
He is the righteous Saviour; and He shall speak Peace unto the Heathen.
[DA CAPO.]

Zechariah 9:9–10 → Matthew 21:5, John 12:15

Paraphrase

Rejoice greatly, O "Daughter of Zion"; shout for joy, O "Daughter of Jerusalem"; look, your king—God's messiah, Jesus—is coming to you: he is the righteous Savior, and he will speak words of peace to the heathen.

Notes:

1. *Zion* is the name for the place where God dwells—formerly, in the Temple, on Mount Zion. The name *Zion* was adopted (NT Hebrews 12:22; Revelation 14:1) for the Christian Church, the place where God dwells now that the Lord God has apparently rejected the Temple.

2. "Daughter of Zion" is an OT name applied to the Christian Church by Jesus' followers (NT Matthew 21:5; John 12:15).

3. OT Zechariah 9:9 is a vexing passage for traditional Christian interpretation. On the face of it, the Hebrew text says not that the king "saves" but that he is "saved." It is of great importance for traditional Christian belief, however, that Zechariah 9:9 be understood to say that the king, God's messiah, is not himself *saved*; the passage needs to carry the meaning, rather, that the king himself actively saves.

Jennens appears to have come up with his own English rendering here, presumably based on the readings of the Latin Bible (i.e., the Vulgate), indebted in turn to the Septuagint reading; and perhaps on the English rendering of the Coverdale Bible and the Bishops' Bible, as well as on the way this verse is given in Edward Chandler's then-well-known book, *A Defence of Christianity, from the Prophecies of the Old Testament* (1725) (see also OT Jeremiah 23:6 and Isaiah 53:11?). Another possibility is that this was Handel's Luther-influenced work, accepted or tolerated by Jennens.

4. The king will speak words of peace to the heathen, that is to say, to the (pagan) gentiles—something that for the (even relatively early on, almost entirely gentile) church was a cause indeed for rejoicing.

OT Zechariah 9:9–10
Rejoice greatly, O daughter of Zion; shout, O daughter of Jerusalem: behold, thy King cometh unto thee: he is just, and having salvation (*KJV marginal note: "Or*, saving himself."), **lowly, and riding upon an ass, and upon a colt the foal of an ass. And I will cut off the chariot from Ephraim, and the horse from Jerusalem, and the battle-bow shall be cut off;** and he shall speak peace unto the

heathen: **and his dominion shall be from sea even to sea, and from the river even to the ends of the** [flat] **earth.**

(See also *Vulgate*, Zechariah 9:9–10
... *iustus et salvator* ... ["(he is) just (i.e., righteous) and
(a) savior," or possibly, "(he is) also (the) righteous savior"].)

(See also *Greek Septuagint*, Zechariah 9:9–10
... [he is] righteous [i.e., Greek: *dikaios*] and saving ...)

(See also *Hebrew Text*, Zechariah 9:9–10
... [he is] righteous and saved ... [*or*, victorious and triumphant].)

(See also Chandler, 1725
Behold thy king cometh unto thee, The righteous one, and that
Savior, lowly and riding upon an Ass ...)

(See also *Coverdale Bible 1535* and *Bishops' Bible 1568*,
Zechariah 9:9
Rejoice thou greatly O daughter Sion, be glad O daughter
Jerusalem: For lo, thy king cometh unto thee, even the righteous
and saviour, lowly and simple is he ...)

(See also *Luther Bible*, Zechariah 9:9–10
Siehe, dein König kommt zu dir, ein Gerechter und ein Helfer ...
["Behold, thy King cometh unto thee, (he is) a righteous man and a
saviour"].)

NT Matthew 21:5
Tell ye the daughter of Sion, Behold, thy King cometh unto thee ...

NT John 12:15
... daughter of Sion: behold, thy King cometh ...

(See also NT 1 John 2:1–2
If any man sin, we have an advocate with the Father, Jesus Christ
the righteous [i.e., Greek: *dikaion*]. And he is the propitiation for
our sins ...)

(See also NT 2 Peter 1:1

. . . to them that have obtained like precious faith with us [i.e., have
obtained a precious faith of the same kind as ours], through the
righteousness of God, and our Saviour Jesus Christ.)

[19] Recit

Then shall the Eyes of the Blind be open'd, and the Ears of the Deaf unstopped; then shall the lame Man leap as a Hart, and the Tongue of the
Dumb shall sing.

Isaiah 35:5–6 → Matthew 11:5, Mark 7:37, Luke 7:22

Paraphrase

*Then, in miracles performed by God's messiah, Jesus, the eyes of
the blind will be opened, and the ears of the deaf will be unblocked;
then the lame man will jump like a deer, and the tongue of the mute
will sing.*

OT Isaiah 35:5–6
Then <u>the eyes of the blind shall</u> be opened, and the ears of the deaf
shall be unstopped. Then shall the lame man leap as <u>an</u> hart, and
the tongue of the <u>dumb sing:</u> **for in the wilderness shall waters
break out, and streams in the desert.**

(See also *Luther Bible*, Isaiah 35:5–6
. . . *und der Stummen Zunge wird Lob sagen* . . . ["and the tongue
of the dumb shall sing praise"].)

(See also Isaiah 35:5–6 in *Kidder*, vol. 1, p. 45
. . . and the tongue of the dumb shall sing.)

NT Matthew 11:5
The blind receive [i.e., from me, Jesus, doing "the works of Christ"—
Matthew 11:2] their sight, and the lame walk, . . . the deaf hear . . .

NT Mark 7:37
He [i.e., Jesus] maketh both the deaf to hear, and the dumb to
speak.

NT Luke 7:22
The blind see, the lame walk, . . . the deaf hear . . .

[20] Song

He shall feed his Flock like a Shepherd: [Handel's setting: *And*] *He shall
gather the Lambs with his Arm, and carry them in his Bosom, and gently lead those that are with young.*

Isaiah 40:11 → [John 10:11]

Paraphrase

*God's messiah, Jesus, will nurture his followers the way a shepherd
feeds his flock: and he will gather the lambs with his arm, carrying
them in his breast, and gently lead those sheep who have young ones.*

OT Isaiah 40:11
He shall feed his flock like a <u>shepherd: he</u> shall gather the lambs
with his arm, and carry them in his bosom, and **shall** gently lead
those that are with young.

(See also NT John 10:11
I [i.e., Jesus] am the good shepherd: the good shepherd giveth his
life for the sheep.)

[20] Song, *continued*

Come unto Him all ye that labour and are heavy laden [Handel's setting:
 *Come unto him, all ye that labour, come unto him all ye that are heavy
 laden*], *and He will give you Rest.*
Take his Yoke upon you, and learn of Him, for He is meek and lowly in
 [Handel's setting: *of*] *Heart: and ye shall find Rest unto your Souls.*

Matthew 11:28–29 ← Jeremiah 6:16

Paraphrase

*Come to him [—believe now in Jesus, God's messiah—] all you who
labor; come to him, all you who are heavily weighed down [with
sin], and he will give you rest [the peace of forgiveness]. Take Jesus'
yoke upon you, and learn from him, because he is gentle and humble-
hearted, and you will find rest for your souls.*

Notes:

1. In a prevalent traditional Christian understanding, "his yoke" is the
easy, gracious yoke of being subjected in faith to God's messiah, Jesus, as
opposed to the difficult, legalistic yoke of Old Israel's Law of Moses (see
also NT Acts 15:10).

NT Matthew 11:28–30 involves an implicit comparison of Moses and
Jesus: Moses is "meek" (OT Numbers 12:3) but apparently brings a relatively difficult "yoke," whereas Jesus is "meek" and brings a relatively easy
"yoke."

At the same time, the call to take on the easy yoke of Jesus in Matthew
11 comes soon after talk of woes to the cities of Chorazin and Bethsaida,
who "did not repent" after witnessing Jesus' "mighty works." The Greek
word underlying *repent* at 11:20 is *metanoeō*. Biblically, a call to this re-

pentance can refer to a total conversion to God or more simply to regret for sin. The former implies inclusion of the latter, of course, but it's the former that seems to be an emphasis of the call in Matthew 11:20–24.

Part 1 of *Messiah* began with explicit talk of sin (i.e., "iniquity," at movement no. 2) and here ends with implicit talk of sin (i.e., leaving the "yoke [of sin]," at nos. 20 to 21). Part 2 begins with a magnificent chorus about Jesus as the Lamb of God that takes away the world's sin.

2. Within the extensive anti-Calvinist writings of eighteenth-century Protestants, this biblical passage (NT Matthew 11:28) was one of the most frequently cited.

Unconditional predestinarians—that is, those who, following Calvinist teaching, believed that God eternally decrees persons to their ultimate ends in heaven or hell, as "elect" or "reprobate"—cited, however, as their coup de grace NT John 6:44 ("No man can come to me [i.e., to Jesus, the Son], except [if God] the Father which hath sent me draw [i.e., impel] him").

NT Matthew 11:28–29
Come unto <u>me</u>, all ye that labour, **and** <u>are</u> heavy laden, and <u>I</u> will give you rest. Take <u>my</u> yoke upon you, and learn of <u>me</u>, for <u>I am</u> meek and lowly in heart: and ye shall find rest unto your souls.

(See also *Luther Bible*, Matthew 11:28–29
. . . *und von Herzen demütig* . . . ["and lowly of heart"].)

OT Jeremiah 6:16
Thus saith the LORD [i.e., to Israel, the people], Stand ye in the ways, and see, and ask for the old paths, where is the good way, and walk therein, and ye shall find rest for your souls: but they said, We will not walk therein.

OT Exodus 33:14
And he [the Lord] said [to Moses], My presence shall go with thee, and I will give thee rest.

(See also OT Numbers 12:3
The man Moses was very meek . . .)

(See also [OT] Sirach 51:23–27

Draw near unto me [i.e., unto Wisdom—what Jesus is implicitly designated in the NT], you unlearned. . . . Put your neck under the yoke [i.e., the yoke of Wisdom], and let your soul receive instruction. . . . Behold with your eyes, how that I have had but little labour, and have gotten unto me much rest.)

(See also NT Acts 15:10

[The apostle Peter said to the apostles and elders gathered in Jerusalem:] Now therefore why tempt ye God, to put a yoke [i.e., the Law of Moses, especially the ritual law of Old Israel] upon the neck of the [gentile] disciples [of Jesus], which neither our fathers [i.e., Old Israel] nor we were able to bear?)

(See also the call of Wisdom, at OT Proverbs 8?)

[21] Chorus

For His Yoke is easy [Handel's setting lacks "For"], *and his Burden is light.*

Matthew 11:30

Paraphrase

Jesus' yoke [unlike Moses's] is easy; and Jesus' burden [unlike Moses's] is light.

Notes:

1. It may be worth noting that in the Gospel of Matthew, Jesus is at times actually depicted as stricter in his requirements than the Law of Moses (see 5:21–22 on murder and anger, and 5:27–28,32 on adultery and lust, and remarriage after divorce).

2. The notion that the Law of Moses, whether its ritual or ethical aspects, was generally considered to be hard or oppressive (see NT Acts 15:10) is not borne out in the Hebrew scriptural or other ancient Jewish texts.

NT Matthew 11:30
For my [i.e., Jesus'] yoke is easy, and my burden is light.

PART TWO

I.
[22] Chorus

Behold the Lamb of God, that taketh away the Sin of the World!

John 1:29 ← [Isaiah 53:7]

Paraphrase

[John the Baptist says:] "Look! This is God's messiah, Jesus, the sacrificial Lamb of God that takes away the sin of the world!"

Notes:

1. Jesus, God's messiah, is called "the Lamb of God" because at his crucifixion he is to be "slaughtered," like the lambs eaten at Israel's yearly festival of Passover, which celebrates her deliverance out of slavery in Egypt (see OT Exodus 12). Jesus even hangs on the cross such that his posture resembles the way Passover lambs were roasted. According to the Gospel of John, Jesus died on the afternoon before the festival started, right as the Passover lambs were slain.

2. Jesus is believed to take away the sin of the world by dying a sacrificial death. Although technically the lamb of the Passover sacrifice was not

a "sin offering," both NT John 1:29 (the libretto's no. 22, here) and Revelation 5:9 (no. 53, below) speak of Jesus as "the Lamb" who is slaughtered as a ransom for sin (see also the OT Isaiah 53:10 of the KJV, but note that the meaning of the Hebrew text here is uncertain).

3. In traditional Christian understandings, only the blood sacrifice of Jesus can substantially effect freedom from sin's bondage; the sin offerings under the now obsolete Law of Moses are mere shadows (or types), not substance (or antitypes).

4. Note that the belief here is that it is sin (i.e., the condition of sinfulness) rather than sins (i.e., individual sinful acts) that the Lamb of God takes away. In this view, people aren't sinners because they sin—they sin because they are sinners. It's from their condition that they need to be "healed."

NT John 1:29
The next day John seeth Jesus coming unto him, and saith, Behold the Lamb of God, <u>which</u> taketh away the sin of the world.

BCP, 1728 [John 1:29]
. . . Lamb of God, that taketh away the sin of the world.

(See also OT Isaiah 53:7
He is brought as a lamb to the slaughter . . .)

(See also NT Hebrews 10:11–14
And every priest [in the Jerusalem Temple] standeth daily ministering and offering oftentimes the same sacrifices, which can never take away sins: but this man [God's messiah, Jesus, the "Lamb of God"; the "high priest of *our* profession"—Hebrews 3:1], after he had offered one sacrifice for sins for ever [in dying on the cross], sat down on [i.e., at] the right hand of God [as predicted at OT Psalm 110:1]; from henceforth expecting till his enemies be made his footstool [as likewise predicted at OT Psalm 110:1]. For by one offering he hath

perfected for ever them that are sanctified [i.e., Jesus' "bretheren" (Hebrews 2:11), his followers, who are healed from sin].)

[23] Song

He was despised and rejected of Men, a Man of Sorrows, and acquainted with Grief.

Isaiah 53:3 → [Matthew 8:17, Mark 9:12]

Paraphrase

[At his crucifixion] God's messiah, Jesus, was despised and rejected by men [particularly, here, by "the Jews"]; Jesus was a man of sorrows, and well familiar with the sickness of humanity's sin.

Notes:

1. Apparently here wishing not to cast aspersions on the followers of Jesus, Jennens omits from his quotation of the prophecy at OT Isaiah 53:3 the words "and we hid as it were our faces from him," and "and we esteemed him not." (See also, however, the libretto's no. 29, below.)

2. At Isaiah 53:3, *grief* is the KJV's translation for the Hebrew word *choliy* ("malady"). The English word *grief* is employed here not in its primary sense of "sadness" but in its less common sense of "sickness." Traditional Christian understandings of the KJV's *grief* as "sickness" would, in any event, be governed by the way OT Isaiah 53:3–4 is quoted at NT Matthew 8:17: "[Jesus] took our infirmities, and bore our sicknesses."

3. Traditionally, Christians have considered Isaiah 53 to be among the most important of the OT texts on messianic expectation. For centuries the

fifteen verses of Isaiah 52:13 to 53:12 have attracted vigorous disagreement among Jewish and Christian interpreters, in particular on the issue
of the identity of Isaiah's "servant" (whom the prophet does not explicitly
associate with God's "anointed one"—i.e., messiah).

Christians typically argue that Isaiah does foretell what happened (as
conveyed in the NT) to the messiah Jesus, who is proclaimed as God's
suffering and atoning servant; and Christians customarily believe that by
simple virtue of the fact that Jesus the Messiah did suffer, Isaiah's predictions have to be read as messianic (as encouraged, to be sure, by NT
Luke 24:25–26). Jews traditionally have seen no reason to link OT Isaiah
52:13–53:12 with God's promised messiah and have read the prophet as
referring not to a single coming figure but to God's servant the people Israel
(as conveyed, for example, at Isaiah 41:8–9), delivered from exile.

> OT Isaiah 53:3
> He is despised and rejected of men; a man of sorrows, and ac-
> quainted with grief: **and we hid as it were our faces from him;** he
> was despised, **and we esteemed him not.**

> (See also NT Mark 9:12
> It is written [i.e., in the OT at Isaiah 53] of the Son of man [i.e.,
> Jesus], that he must suffer many things, and be set at nought.)

> (See also NT Matthew 8:17
> He [i.e., Jesus] . . . healed all that were sick, that it might be fulfilled
> which was spoken by Esaias the prophet [i.e., at OT Isaiah 53:3–4],
> saying, Himself took our infirmities, and bore our sicknesses [i.e.,
> traditionally, Jesus is believed to have fulfilled these words of Isaiah
> 53 in the highest sense, by eventually bearing humanity's sins in
> his own body, suffering on the cross; in a lower sense, by presently
> sympathizing with his followers in their sorrows, and healing their
> diseases, the fruit of original sin].)

> (See also NT Luke 24:25–27 and Acts 2:32–35.)

[23] Song, *continued*

---

*He gave his Back to the Smiters, and his Cheeks to them that plucked off
the Hair: He hid not his Face from Shame and Spitting.* [DA CAPO.]

Isaiah 50:6 → Matthew 26:67, 27:26

Paraphrase

*God's messiah, Jesus, before his crucifixion, offered his bare back to
those [the Jewish councilors and Roman soldiers] who tortured him,
and offered his cheeks to those who pulled out his beard: he didn't
hide his face from shame and spitting in his face [by "the Jews"].*

Note:

At the NT passion narrative, Jesus offers his back to "the Jews," and
through them, to Pilate, the Roman governor. According to Matthew
26:67, it is only Jews who spit explicitly "in his face" (whereas at 27:30 it
says that Romans spit generally "upon him").

In a strict typological Christian understanding of OT Isaiah 50, Jesus
will likewise have offered his cheeks to those (Jews or Romans, or both?)
who pull out his beard, although—perhaps surprisingly—the NT does not
make any mention of this extraordinary narrative event.

OT Isaiah 50:6
I gave my back to the smiters, and my cheeks to them that plucked
off the hair: I hid not my face from shame and spitting.

NT Matthew 26:67, 27:26
Then did they [i.e., "the Jews" of the council] spit in his [i.e., Jesus']
face, and buffeted him; and others smote him [i.e., Jesus] with the

palms of their hands . . . and when he [i.e., Pilate, the Roman gov-
ernor] had scourged Jesus [i.e., beat him with a whip], he delivered
him to be crucified.

[24] Chorus

Surely He hath born our Griefs, and carried our Sorrows:
He was wounded for our Transgressions, He was bruised for our Iniquities;
the Chastisement of our Peace was upon Him,

Isaiah 53:4–5a → Matthew 8:10–12,17

Paraphrase

On the cross, Jesus, God's messiah, certainly has borne our [his follow-
ers'] sicknesses, our sins; and certainly has carried our [guilt-induced]
sorrows; Jesus was wounded because of our transgressions, our sin; he
was crushed because of our iniquities; on him was the punishment [his
sacrificial death on the cross] that brought us [his followers] peace.

Notes:

1. At the previous verse, OT Isaiah 53:3, *grief* is the KJV's translation for
the Hebrew word *choliy* ("malady"). The English word *grief* is employed here
not in its primary sense of "sadness" but in its less common sense of "sickness." Traditional Christian understandings of the KJV's *grief* as "sickness"
would, in any event, be governed by the way OT Isaiah 53:3–4 is quoted at
NT Matthew 8:17, "[Jesus] took our infirmities, and bore our sicknesses."

2. In traditional understandings, Jesus' sacrificial death brings peace to
his followers, the *spiritual* children of Abraham. The crucifixion of Jesus
does not, of course, bring peace to the *natural* children of Abraham who

don't believe in Jesus, namely "the Jews" (on this, see NT Matthew 8:12, as cited two paragraphs below).

OT Isaiah 53:4–5a
Surely he hath born our griefs, and carried our sorrows: **yet we did esteem him stricken, smitten of God, and afflicted. But** he was wounded for our transgressions, he was bruised for our iniquities: the chastisement of our peace was upon him,

NT Matthew 8:10–12,17
[At his healing of a centurion's servant,] Jesus said to them that followed [him], ". . . many [i.e., many gentiles, who are believers in Jesus, God's messiah] shall [i.e., in the end] come from the east and west, and shall sit down with Abraham, and Isaac, and Jacob [the three of whom are proto-Christians], in the kingdom of heaven: but the children of the kingdom [i.e., the natural children of Abraham who don't believe in Jesus, namely "the Jews": "the children of the earthly kingdom"—as opposed to the spiritual children of Abraham, namely the followers of Jesus] shall be cast out into outer darkness . . ." [and later, on the evening of his having healed his disciple Peter's mother-in-law] he [Jesus] . . . healed all that were sick, that it might be fulfilled which was spoken by Esaias the prophet [i.e., at OT Isaiah 53:3–4], saying, Himself took our infirmities, and bore our sicknesses [i.e., the "griefs" that are the fruit of original sin].

NT Romans 4:24–25
. . . if we believe on him that raised up Jesus our Lord . . . who was delivered for our offences . . .

NT 1 Corinthians 15:1–3
I [i.e., Paul the apostle] declare to you [i.e., to you believers in Jesus] . . . Christ died for our sins according to the scriptures . . .

NT Romans 5:1–2
We have peace with God through our Lord Jesus Christ. By whom we have access by faith . . .

[25] [Chorus]

---

and with His Stripes we are healed.

Isaiah 53:5b → 1 Peter 2:24

Paraphrase

And with the blood-welts of Jesus', God's messiah's, flogging bruises, on the cross, we [followers of Jesus] are healed of our sickness: sin. [We, the followers of Jesus, are saved.]

Notes:

1. Appropriate to the sense—as governed by the quotation of this text from OT Isaiah 53 at NT 1 Peter 2—that the *we* who "are/were healed" are the followers of Jesus ("the bishop of [our] souls"), Handel musically sets this text exclusively in the *stylus ecclesiasticus*, the "church style" (i.e., a traditional language, reminiscent of the great renaissance composer Palestrina, in which all the lines in the texture are melodic in character, featuring staggered imitative entries of "vocal melody"—as opposed to "instrumental melody"—and a strict avoidance of dance rhythms).

2. Typically in traditional Christian understandings, *we*, Jesus' followers, alone "are healed" (NT 1 Peter 2:24) by the "stripes" of his life-giving blood. Even if Jesus died for everyone, he did not *save* everyone.

OT Isaiah 53:5b
and with his stripes we are healed.

NT 1 Peter 2:24
Who his own self [i.e., Jesus] bore our sins in his own body on the tree [i.e., the cross; see also OT Deuteronomy 21:23], that we, being

dead to sin, should live unto righteousness: by whose stripes ye [i.e., you followers of Jesus] were healed [i.e., "saved"].

[26] Chorus

All we, like Sheep, have gone astray [Handel's setting: *All we like sheep, all we like sheep have gone astray*], *we have turned every one to his own Way, and the Lord hath laid on Him the Iniquity of us all.*

Isaiah 53:6 → 1 Peter 2:25

Paraphrase

All of us [emphatically, the followers of Jesus[6]] have been like lost sheep, going dangerously astray, each on our own path [until we are returned to the "Shepherd of our souls," Jesus]; and the Lord God has laid on Jesus the iniquity of all of us [by ordaining Jesus' sacrificial death on the cross].

Note:

Handel's chorus delivers the words "All we like sheep" not only in an uninflected manner but also musically separated from "have gone astray." For the 1743 wordbook of *Messiah*, Jennens may have changed the KJV's "All we like sheep have gone astray" to "All we, like sheep, have gone astray" with the hope of discouraging audiences from hearing Handel's chorus as proclaiming that believers in Jesus are fond of sheep. (Handel's setting of the opening phrase has been the bane of choral conductors for generations.)

OT Isaiah 53:6
All we like sheep have gone astray: we have turned every one to his own way, and the LORD hath laid on him the iniquity of us all.

NT 1 Peter 2:25

For ye [i.e., you followers of Jesus, the "you which believe" of 1 Peter 2:7] were as sheep going astray, but are now returned unto the Shepherd and Bishop of your souls [i.e., by the crucifixion of Jesus].

[27] Recit accomp

All they that see him laugh him to scorn; they shoot out their Lips, and shake their Heads, saying,

Psalm 22:7 → Matthew 27:39–40

Paraphrase

All of them [here, namely, the Jewish persons⁷ witnessing Jesus' execution] laugh him to scorn; they curl their [blasphemous] lips, and shake their heads, saying,

[this biblical passage continues at the next movement, the libretto's no. 28]

Note:

"All they" cannot refer to all humanity. The followers of Jesus in NT Matthew 27, where this text is quoted, did not laugh him to scorn. Indeed, it's virtually unimaginable that any follower of Jesus would ever do so, then or later. And gentile unbelievers, perhaps needless to say, would not speak the words of the libretto's no. 28, below (or of NT Matthew 27:40).

BCP 1728 Psalm 22:7

All they that see <u>me</u>, laugh <u>me</u> to scorn: they shoot out their lips, and shake their heads, saying,

OT Psalm 22:7

All they that see <u>me</u> laugh <u>me</u> to scorn: they shoot out <u>the lip, they shake the head</u>, saying,

NT Matthew 27:39–40

And they [i.e., the Jewish pilgrims attending Passover] that passed by, reviled him [i.e., Jesus, on the cross], wagging their heads, and saying, Thou that destroyest the temple, and buildest it in three days, save thyself. If thou be the Son of God, come down from the cross.

[28] Chorus

He trusted in God, that He would [Handel's setting, sometimes: *might*] *deliver him: Let him deliver him, if he delight in him.*

Psalm 22:8 → Matthew 27:43

Paraphrase

[this biblical passage continues from the previous movement, the libretto's no. 27]

"Jesus trusted in God, confident that God would rescue him: let God rescue Jesus from the cross, if indeed God takes delight in him."

Note:

In contrast to the libretto's no. 25, "And with His Stripes we are healed," which was set musically in the church style, no. 28 is set in the aggressive style of so-called *turba* choruses, the more turbulent "crowd" numbers that are found in contemporaneous musical settings of the passion narrative.

This is the style employed, for example, when the chorus of Jews in Bach's *St. Matthew Passion* exclaims, "Er hat Gott vertrauet, der erlöse ihn nun, lüstets ihn" ("He trusted in God—who may redeem him now, should He desire him"), and also when *das Volk* ("the people"—Luther's misrendering of Matthew's expression "the [ethnically mixed] crowds") shout out concerning Jesus, "Laß ihn kreuzigen!" ("Have him crucified!").

BCP 1728, Psalm 22:8
He trusted in God, that he would deliver him: let him deliver him, if he will have him.

OT Psalm 22:8
He trusted on the LORD, that he would deliver him: let him deliver him seeing he delighted in him. [*KJV marginal note:* "*Or*, if he delight in him."]

Wells, Psalm 22:8
He trusted on the Lord, that he would deliver him: let him deliver him, if he delight in him.

(See also *Luther Bible*, Matthew 27:43
... *Er hat* GOTT *vertrauet, der erlöse ihn nun* ... ["he trusted in God, who may (*or*, might) redeem him now"].)

NT Matthew 27:43
[i.e., in Matthew, the Jewish leaders—the chief priests, scribes, and elders—likewise exclaim mockingly, concerning Jesus on the cross:] He trusted in God; let him deliver him now, if he will have him ...

[29] Recit accomp

Thy Rebuke hath broken his Heart; He is full of Heaviness: He looked for some to have Pity on him, but there was no Man, neither found he any to comfort him.

Psalm 69:20

Paraphrase

Your harsh reproach, God, [in afflicting Jesus with the cross,] has broken his heart; Jesus is fraught with dejection: he looked for some to take pity on him at his crucifixion, but there was no one; he didn't find anyone who would comfort him, either.

Notes:

1. The word *thy* in "Thy rebuke" appears in the BCP but not in the KJV or in other standard Bibles. Jennens's *thy* can't refer (prophetically) to the Jewish passersby of the passion narrative, because the word *thy* is singular, not plural. In older English *thou* and *thy* are singular, whereas *ye* and *your* are plural, the latter also being used for collective nouns (e.g., for the house of Israel). The plural forms *ye* and *your* were used also for (formally) addressing an individual human superior, but not for addressing Jesus, or God "the Father." It is widely believed today that *thou* is formal usage (i.e., because it is now experienced as dignified) and *you* informal, but historically in fact it was the other way around: people addressed God informally with *thou*, just as German speakers still today address God with the informal *Du* form but address human superiors with the (otherwise plural) formal *Sie* form.

And so, "*Thy* rebuke" must mean God's rebuke. Had the text been meant to refer to those people witnessing Jesus' crucifixion, it would have read "Your rebuke." (This would be the first time God is addressed in the libretto; God is clearly addressed with *thou* and *thy* at the libretto's nos. 31 and 32, below.)

To accommodate its application to the NT passion narrative, Jennens did change the other pronouns of Psalm 69 from first-person singular (*I, me, my*) to third-person singular (*he, him, his*), but he did not change the BCP's second-person singular informal pronoun (*thy*) to the second-person plural (*your*).

Though Jesus is depicted in Matthew's passion narrative as crying out to God from the cross (quoting OT Psalm 22:1) "my God, my God, why hast thou forsaken me?" it may be hard to believe that God could be taken to have "*broken his* [Jesus'] *heart*." Newton's *Discourses on Messiah*, for example, does however speak here untroubledly of God "the Holy Father" breaking Jesus' heart; Newton explains that Jesus is "treated as [if he were] a sinner."

2. In its original historical context, the *I* of this Psalm is apparently an individual who is lamenting the Temple destruction of 586 BCE and is widely reviled for it (see OT Psalm 69:10; see also NT John 2:17).

BCP 1728, Psalm 69:21

Thy rebuke hath broken <u>my</u> heart; <u>I am</u> full of heaviness: <u>I</u> looked for some to have pity on <u>me</u>, but there was no man, neither found <u>I</u> any to comfort <u>me</u>.

OT Psalm 69:20

<u>Reproach</u> hath broken <u>my</u> heart; **and** <u>I am</u> full of heaviness: **and** <u>I</u> looked for some to <u>take pity</u>, but there was <u>none; and for comfort-ers, but I found none</u>.

(OT Psalm 69 is much alluded to in the NT passion narratives; see also OT Lamentations 1:12c.)

[30] Song

Behold, and see, if there be any Sorrow like unto His Sorrow!

Lamentations 1:12

Paraphrase

Look, and see if there is any sorrow that approaches Jesus' sorrow on the cross!

Notes:

1. This text is taken to be predictive of Jesus' sorrow on the cross, where the Lamb of God's suffering is unlike any other human suffering, as it

involves not only the excruciating physical pain of crucifixion but also the overwhelming experience of bearing the world's sin.

2. In its historical context, this poetry from the book of Lamentations weeps over the destruction of Jerusalem and its Temple in 586 BCE.

This text is recited, as it was in Handel's day, in the synagogue on Tishah B'Av, a day of public mourning and fasting that commemorates the destructions of the Temple in 586 BCE and 70 CE. According to traditional histories, England's Jews were expelled (in 1290 CE) on Tishah B'Av. Only centuries later were Jews allowed again to live in England.

Lamentations is well known from the Catholic liturgy's magnificent musical use of it on the Thursday, Friday, and Saturday of Holy Week, preceding Easter Sunday.

In Handel's day the Church of England annually recited the whole book of Lamentations, divided into certain lessons for morning prayer or evening prayer on 12–14 August.

OT Lamentations 1:12

Is it nothing to you, all ye that pass by? behold and see, if there be any sorrow like unto <u>my</u> sorrow, **which is done unto me, wherewith the** Lord **hath afflicted me, in the day of his fierce anger.**

(For OT Lamentations 1:12a, see also NT Matthew 27:39, "And they [i.e., the Jewish pilgrims attending Passover] that passed by, reviled him [i.e., Jesus, on the cross] . . .)

II.

[31] Recit accomp

He was cut off out of the Land of the Living: For the Transgression of thy People was He stricken.

Isaiah 53:8

Paraphrase

Jesus was violently put to death: For the transgression, God, of your people was Jesus struck down.

OT Isaiah 53:8

He was taken from prison and from judgment: and who shall de-clare his generation? for he was cut off out of the land of the living: for the transgression of <u>my</u> people was he stricken.

(For parallel to OT Isaiah 53:7–8a, see NT Acts 8:32–33.)

[32] Song

But Thou didst not leave his Soul in Hell, nor didst Thou suffer thy Holy One to see Corruption.

Psalm 16:10 → Acts 2:27,31; 13:35

Paraphrase

But you, God, didn't leave Jesus' soul in Hades; nor did you allow the body of your Holy One, Jesus, to decay.

Notes:

1. The "hell" that OT Psalm 16 speaks of in the libretto's no. 32 is Sheol or Hades, the grave in which after death the "soul" (biblical Greek, *psychē*) stays temporarily, without the (rest of the) "body" (biblical Greek, *sōma*)—unlike the hell Gehenna, where the "souls" of the ungodly will stay definitively, along with their resurrected "bodies." Regarding the biblical body and soul, see also the extensive note on the libretto's no. 45, below.

2. The libretto's no. 32 does not concern the controversial doctrine of the harrowing of hell, according to which Jesus, between his burial and resurrection, overcame Hell (the place where *all* pre-Christian humanity will have faced punishment on account of original sin), freeing its captives, above all Adam and Eve, as well as the righteous, messiah-expecting Israelites of OT times.

Jennens and his fellow members of the Church of England held that OT Psalm 16:10—as well as the Apostles' Creed (". . . [Jesus] descended into hell; the third day he rose again from the dead . . .")—referred not to this contested doctrine but simply to Jesus' descent into the hell Sheol (Hades).

BCP 1728, Psalm 16:11
For why? thou shalt not leave my soul in hell: neither shalt thou suffer thy holy One to see corruption.

OT Psalm 16:10
For thou wilt not leave my soul in hell; neither wilt thou suffer thine holy One to see corruption.

NT Acts 2:27,31
[i.e., Jesus' disciple Peter, speaking to the "men of Israel," reports that King David, the writer of psalms, said predictively of Jesus:] Because thou wilt not leave my soul in hell [i.e., in the grave—the "hell" Hades (Sheol)], neither wilt thou suffer [i.e., allow] thine holy One to see corruption [i.e., bodily decay]. . . . He [i.e., David, at Psalm 16] seeing this before, spake of the resurrection of Christ, that his soul was not left in hell, neither his flesh did see corruption.

NT Acts 13:35
[Says the apostle Paul to those assembled in a synagogue at Antioch in Pisidia:] Wherefore he [i.e., King David] saith also in another psalm, Thou [i.e., God] shalt not suffer thine holy One [i.e., Jesus] to see corruption.

III.

[33] Chorus and/or Semichorus

Lift up your Heads, O ye Gates, and be ye lift up, ye everlasting Doors, and the King of Glory shall come in.

Who is this King of Glory?

The Lord Strong and Mighty; the Lord Mighty in Battle.

Lift up your Heads, O ye Gates, and be ye lift up, ye everlasting Doors, and the King of Glory shall come in.

Who is this King of Glory?

The Lord of Hosts: He is the King of Glory.

[Handel's setting, extra:] *The Lord of Hosts: He is the King of Glory.*

Psalm 24:7–10

Paraphrase

Raise your heads, O you gates of heaven, and be raised, you everlasting doors, and the King of Glory—God's messiah, Jesus—will come in, to enter heaven [where he will rule at the right hand of God]. [The angels shout out:] "Who is this King of Glory?" The response: "The Lord strong and powerful; the Lord, Jesus, who is powerful in battle [against sin and evil]." Raise your heads, O you gates of heaven, and be raised, you everlasting doors, and the King of Glory—God's messiah, Jesus—will come in, to enter heaven. [The angels shout out again:] "Who is this King of Glory?" The response: "The Lord God of Heavenly Armies of angels, who surround God's throne. This Lord is Jesus [God the Son—of one Being with "God the Father," who is likewise called the Lord of Heavenly Armies]: he, Jesus, is the King of Glory."

Notes:

1. Traditionally, Christians have read this poetry as foreshadowing the resurrected Jesus' entering heaven to sit at the right hand of God.

The text is extremely prevalent in Judaism, as traditionally it is recited in the liturgy on festivals, when Torah scrolls are returned to "the Ark [for the Torah]" at the front of the synagogue. In pre-Christian times, Psalm 24:7–10 was meant to mark the liturgical entrance of the Ark of the Covenant into the Temple.

2. The meaning of the "heads" in the Hebrew phrase *seu shearim rasheichem* here at Psalm 24:7 is unclear. It might refer to the upper wings of the sanctuary's gates, or to the horizontal crossbeam of the gate area.

BCP 1728, Psalm 24:7–10
Lift up your heads, O ye gates, and be ye lift up, ye everlasting doors: and the King of glory shall come in. Who is the King of glory: it is the Lord strong and mighty, even the Lord mighty in battle. Lift up your heads, O ye gates, and be ye lift up, ye everlasting doors: and the King of glory shall come in. Who is the King of glory: even the Lord of hosts, he is the King of glory.

OT Psalm 24:7–10
Lift up your heads, O ye gates; and be ye lift up, ye everlasting doors, and the King of glory shall come in. Who is this King of glory? The LORD strong and mighty, the LORD mighty in battle. Lift up your heads, O ye gates, even lift them up, ye everlasting doors, and the King of glory shall come in. Who is this King of glory? The LORD of hosts, he is the King of glory. Selah.

(See also NT James 2:1
My brethren, have not the faith of our Lord Jesus Christ, the Lord of glory, with respect of persons.)

(See also NT Revelation 21:10–14
And he [i.e., one of the seven angels of the seven churches in Asia: at Ephesus, Smyrna, Pergamos, Thyatira, Sardis, Philadelphia, and

Laodicea] . . . shewed me [i.e., John, the author of Revelation] that
great city, the holy Jerusalem, descending out of heaven from God,
having the glory of God . . . and had . . . twelve gates, and at the
gates twelve angels . . . and the wall of the city [i.e., the new, heavenly Jerusalem] had twelve foundations, and in them the names of
the twelve apostles [i.e., the twelve disciples of Jesus' inner circle] of
the Lamb [i.e., of Jesus, the "Lamb of God"].)

IV.

[34] Recit

Unto which of the Angels said He at any time, Thou art my Son, this Day
have I begotten thee?

Hebrews 1:5 ← Psalm 2:7

Paraphrase

*To which of the angels did God ever say, as God did of Jesus, "You
are my Son; on this day have I begotten you"?*

Notes:

1. "On this day" here means a day just like the day of Jesus' resurrection, when God declares Jesus to be God's Son in a sort of second birth,
out of Mother Earth, the grave. Interpreters traditionally speak of God's
(temporal) announcement of Christ's Sonship. They needn't see a contra-
diction in the fact that Jesus Christ is understood to be "eternally begotten
of [God] the Father" (as the Nicene Creed states), that is, that he can't have
been literally "begotten" on a particular day.

2. "This day have I begotten thee" at Psalm 2:7 may originally have meant simply "this day you have been enthroned."

NT Hebrews 1:5

For unto which of the angels said he at any time, Thou art my Son, this day have I begotten thee? **And again, I will be to him a Father, and he shall be to me a Son?**

OT Psalm 2:7

Thou art my Son; this day have I begotten thee.

(For parallel to NT Hebrews 1:5b, see also OT 2 Samuel 7:14.)

(See also NT Acts 13:32–33

And we [i.e., both the apostle, Paul, and his assistant, Barnabus] declare [in the synagogue at Antioch in Pisidia] unto you [i.e., to "the Jews," most of whom did not believe Paul's preaching, and to the gentile "god-fearers" (sympathizers with Judaism), many of whom did believe Paul's good news about Jesus] glad tidings, how that the promise [i.e., of the coming of God's messiah] which was made unto the fathers, God hath fulfilled the same unto us their children, in that he hath raised up Jesus again, as it is also written in the second Psalm: Thou art my Son, this day have I begotten thee.)

[35] Chorus

Let all the Angels of God worship Him.

Hebrews 1:6 ← Psalm 97:7

Paraphrase

[God exhorts concerning the "first-begotten into the world," Jesus:]
"Let all the angels of God in heaven worship Jesus."

Note:

At NT Hebrews 1–2 the author is emphasizing that Jesus is the "first-begotten" Son of God and thus superior to the angels (i.e., he is not just another *aggelos* [messenger or angel] of God, nor is he a "mere" human creature); he deserves to be worshiped by the angels of God.

NT Hebrews 1:6
And again, when he bringeth in the first-begotten into the world, he saith, And let all the angels of God worship him.

OT Psalm 97:7
. . . worship him, all ye gods.

(See also *Greek Septuagint*, Psalm 96:7
. . . worship him, all ye his angels.)

(See also *Greek Septuagint*, Deuteronomy 32:43
. . . let all the sons of God worship him.)

(See also Hebrew–Dead Sea Scroll, Deuteronomy 32:43
. . . worship him, o every god!)

V.

[36] Song

Thou art gone up on High; Thou hast led Captivity captive, and received Gifts for Men, yea, even for thine Enemies, that the Lord God might dwell among them.

Psalm 68:18 → Ephesians 4:7–8

Paraphrase

You, Jesus, are gone up on high, into heaven; you have taken captivity itself captive, and you have received gifts [namely, the gifts of the "unity

*of the faith and of the knowledge of the Son of God"] from God to give
to humanity, yes indeed, even to your enemies [namely, the unbelieving
Jews and pagans], so that the Lord God might dwell among them.*

Notes:

1. In traditional Christian understandings, Jesus' entering heaven and
"leading captivity captive" means that Jesus has taken captive the curse of
the now obsolete Law of Moses, and of sin and death.

Technically, the curse of the Law results from the guilt incurred by dis-
obedience to the Law of Moses. The apostle Paul gives a complex and
subtle explanation in the book of Romans, in which he holds that the Law
is itself good ("Wherefore the law is holy, and the commandment holy, and
just, and good," Romans 7:12), though, in a sense, it brings the cognizance
of sin into the world and, thus, indirectly brings sin "to life" (7:7–14).

2. In traditional Christian understandings, Jesus' enemies, here (OT
Psalm 68 and NT Ephesians 4), are the unbelieving Jews and pagans who
may yet receive the saving gifts of the "unity of the [Christian] faith, and of
the knowledge of the Son of God" (Ephesians 4:13—after having quoted,
at 4:8, the text of Psalm 68:18). More fully, the gifts of Christ are listed
at Ephesians 4:11–13 as: "And he [Christ] gave some, apostles; and some,
prophets; and some, evangelists; and some, pastors and teachers; for the
perfecting of the saints, for the work of the ministry, for the edifying of the
body of Christ [i.e., for the edifying of the Christian Church]: till we all
come in the unity of the faith, and of the knowledge of the Son of God, unto
a perfect man, unto the measure of the stature of the fullness of Christ."

3. "That the Lord God might dwell among them" is traditionally taken
to mean something like: "so that, in a rebellious world, Jesus might set up
his church, replacing the Temple, as the place where God dwells."

BCP 1728, Psalm 68:18
Thou art gone up on high, thou hast led captivity captive, and received gifts for men: yea, even for thine enemies, that the Lord God
might dwell among them.

OT Psalm 68:18

Thou <u>hast ascended</u> on high, thou hast led captivity captive: **thou hast** received gifts for men (*KJV marginal note: "Heb[rew].* <u>in the man</u>"); yea, <u>for the rebellious also</u>, that the LORD God might dwell among them.

NT Ephesians 4:7–8

But unto every one of us [i.e., us followers of Jesus] is given grace according to the measure of the gift of Christ. Wherefore he [i.e., this is why David, the psalmist] saith [at Psalm 68:18], When he ascended up on high, he led captivity captive, and gave gifts unto men.

(See also NT Colossians 2:15.)

[37] Chorus

The Lord gave the Word: Great was the Company of the Preachers.

Psalm 68:11

Paraphrase

The Lord God gave the command [to spread the good news of Jesus], and the regiment of preachers of the gospel was very large.

Note:

In traditional Christian understandings of OT Psalm 16, the Lord God commands believers in God's messiah, Jesus, to spread the gospel among all nations on earth, to the gentiles and Diaspora Jews.

BCP 1728, Psalm 68:11
The Lord gave the word: great was the company of the preachers.

OT Psalm 68:11
The Lord gave the word: great was the company of <u>those that published it</u>.

(See also NT Luke 24:47
Repentance and remission of sins should be preached in his [i.e., Jesus Christ's] name among all nations. . . .)

[38a/b, 38e] Song

[One of Handel's settings: *How beautiful are the Feet of them that preach the Gospel of Peace, and bring glad Tidings of good Things.*]

Romans 10:15 ← Isaiah 52:7,9

Paraphrase

How exquisitely timely are the feet of them who preach the gospel—the good news—of the spiritual peace that God's messiah, Jesus, affords; and who bring happy news of good things.

Note:

In traditional Christian understandings, the "glad tidings" and "good things" of NT Romans 10:15 refer to eternal salvation in Jesus.

NT Romans 10:15
And how shall they preach, except they be sent? as it is written,
How beautiful are the feet of them that preach the gospel of peace, and bring glad tidings of good things!

OT Isaiah 52:7
How beautiful upon the mountains are the feet of him that bringeth
good tidings, that publisheth peace; that bringeth good tidings of
good, that publisheth salvation; that saith unto Zion, Thy God
reigneth!

OT Nahum 1:15
Behold upon the mountains the feet of him that bringeth good
tidings, that publisheth peace: O Judah, keep thy solemn feasts,
perform thy vows: for the wicked [*KJV marginal note: "Heb(rew).*
Belial."] shall no more pass through thee, he is utterly cut off.

or [38c/38d] Duet & Chorus

How beautiful are the Feet of them [Handel's settings: or, *him*] *that bring*
[Handel's settings: or, *bringeth*] *good* [Handel's settings: *or, glad*] *Tid-*
ings, Tidings of Salvation; that say [Handel's settings: or, *saith*] *unto Sion,*
thy God reigneth, break forth into Joy, glad Tidings, thy God reigneth!

Isaiah 52:7,9 ↔ Romans 10:15

Paraphrase

How exquisitely timely are the feet of them, the preachers, who bring
happy news: news of salvation; how exquisitely timely are the feet of
them who say to Zion, "Your God—Jesus—reigns; break out with
shouts of joy—happy news—your God reigns!

Notes:

1. In traditional Christian readings, the "tidings . . . of salvation" at OT
Isaiah 52:7 refer to eternal salvation in Jesus, God's messiah.

2. *Zion* is the name for the place where God dwells—formerly, in the Temple, on Mount Zion. The name *Zion* was adopted (NT Hebrews 12:22; Revelation 14:1) for the Christian Church, the place where God dwells now that the Lord God has apparently rejected the Temple.

OT Isaiah 52:7,9
How beautiful **upon the mountains** are the feet of him that bringeth good tidings, **that publisheth peace, that bringeth good** tidings of **good, that publisheth** salvation, that saith unto Zion, Thy God reigneth! [. . .] Break forth into joy, **sing together, ye waste places of Jerusalem: for the** Lord **hath comforted his people, he hath redeemed Jerusalem.**

NT Romans 10:15
And how shall they [i.e., how shall anyone] preach, except they be sent? as it is written, How beautiful are the feet of them that preach the gospel of peace, and bring glad tidings of good things!

(For parallel to OT Isaiah 52:7b, see also NT Ephesians 6:15.)

NT Romans 10:15b
How beautiful are the feet of them that **preach the gospel of peace, and** bring glad tidings **of good things!**

OT Isaiah 52:7
How beautiful upon the mountains are the feet of him that bringeth good tidings, that publisheth peace; that bringeth good tidings of good, that publisheth salvation; that saith unto Zion, Thy God reigneth!

[39, *or* end of 38b] Chorus, *or* Song

Their Sound is gone out into all Lands, and their Words unto the Ends of the World.

Psalm 19:4 ↔ Romans 10:18

Paraphrase

Their sound [the sounding of the gospel-preaching voices] is gone out into all lands, and their words toward the outermost parts of the [flat] world.

Note:

The libretto combines the wordings of OT Psalm 19:4 and NT Romans 10:18. The Psalm is quoted in Romans to indicate that Old Israel has had plenty of opportunity to hear the good news of salvation in God's messiah: Jesus. That is to say, unbelief in Jesus—and in particular the obstinacy of Jewish unbelief—cannot be blamed on lack of opportunity to hear the gospel. The book of Romans (i.e., 11:26) also, however, envisages the inclusion, in the end, of "all Israel" in God's salvation.

BCP 1728 Psalm 19:4–5
Their sound is gone out into all lands: and their words <u>into</u> the ends of the world. **In them hath he set a tabernacle for the sun.**

OT Psalm 19:4
Their <u>line</u> is gone out <u>through</u> all <u>the earth</u>, and their words <u>to</u> the ends of the world: **in them hath he set a tabernacle for the sun.**

NT Romans 10:18
But I [i.e., Paul] **say, Have they** [i.e., especially Israel] **not heard? Yes verily,** their [i.e., here: the gospel preachers'] sound <u>went</u> into all <u>the earth,</u> and their words unto the ends of the world.

VI.
[40] Song

Why do the Nations so furiously rage together? and why do the People imagine a vain Thing?

The Kings of the Earth rise up, and the Rulers take Counsel [Handel's setting, sometimes: *"Counsels"*] *together against the Lord and against his
Anointed.*

Psalm 2:1–2 → Acts 4:24–28

Paraphrase

Why do the nations *[the Romans and Jews] so furiously rage together
[against Jesus]? And why do* the people *[of Israel, "the Jews"] con-
template an idle thing [namely, the notion of prevailing against God's
Anointed One, Christ Jesus, and against his message]? The earthly
kings [the Jewish tetrarch, Herod; and the Roman governor, Pilate]
rise up, and the rulers [the Sanhedrin of "the Jews"] take counsel
together, against the Lord God and against God's Anointed [namely,
the messiah, Jesus].*

Notes:

1. Jennens's change from the KJV and BCP's rendering *heathen* to the
word *nations* allows those-who-rage to include the nation of Old Israel
("the Jews") along with the heathen. ("The Jews" are not "heathen.") Thus,
if in the KJV of OT Psalm 2:1–2, "the Jews" will simply imagine a vain
thing against Jesus, in *Messiah* "the Jews" will also furiously rage with
violence against Jesus. "The Jews," in particular, will rage against Jesus,
leading to his crucifixion, in the NT passion narratives; and "the Jews,"
in particular, will rage against the preaching of his gospel, at NT Acts 1–4
(which quotes OT Psalm 2 in this connection).

2. The idea in the earlier historical contexts of Psalm 2 ("why do the
goyim . . . and why do the *lehummim*") is that neither the *goyim* nations
nor the *lehummim* peoples are Israelites; that is to say, both groups who
torment God's anointed one, here understood to be King David of Israel,
are decidedly non-"Jews."

The question is, to whom would *goyim* refer in a prophetic reading of the psalm? Some will raise the objection that no matter how Jennens translated *goyim*, he can't ever have imagined *Jews* to be included among the prophetic *goyim* here at the libretto's no. 40, because Jennens must have known that the word *goyim* always means non-Jews. But the definition of *goyim* as exclusively "non-Jews" is correct only in postbiblical parlance.

Jennens, an accomplished student of the Bible, will probably have known that in the Hebrew text of the OT the Israelites are in fact at times referred to with the words *goy* and *goyim*. (See, e.g., OT Genesis 48:19, "[Jacob-cum-Israel's grandson Ephraim's] offspring will become a multitude of the nations [*melo ha-goyim*]; and OT Exodus 19:6, "You [the Israelites] shall be for me [the Lord God] a priestly kingdom and a holy nation [a *goy kadosh*]"; see also, however, OT Numbers 23:9.)

3. In traditional Christian understandings (as governed by NT Acts 4:24–28, which quotes OT Psalm 2 and identifies its "the people" as "the people of Israel," namely "the Jews"), "Why do the people imagine a vain thing?" means: Why do "the Jews" think they can ultimately prevail against Jesus and his message, the gospel?

4. In traditional Christian interpretation, "the kings of the earth" are Herod Antipas—the (believed-to-be-Jewish) tetrarch of Galilee, son of Herod the Great (who was called King of the Jews)—along with Pilate, the Roman governor of Judea, who is representative of the "king," Caesar.

5. In traditional Christian understandings, "the rulers" are the Sanhedrin—the leaders of the people, of Old Israel, "the Jews."

6. The kings and rulers take counsel against God's messiah—in Hebrew, *mashiyach*; in Greek, *Christos*; in literal English translation, *Anointed One*.

Broader Note:

Jennens's use and placement of OT Psalm 2 here—rather than at the libretto's passion-narrative section—is evidently governed not by the reading of Psalm 2 in the Easter liturgy of the Church of England but by the extensive quotation of Psalm 2 in the (post-Easter) biblical narrative of NT

Acts 1–4, where Jesus' disciples, like here in *Messiah*, go out among the nations to preach the gospel, meeting much hostility from Jews—just the sort of treatment that Jesus himself had frequently met from Jews in his earthly ministry, according to the NT gospel accounts.

At this post-Easter portion of *Messiah*, just like in the narrative of NT Acts 1–4, the libretto is apparently designed (by citing the prophetic OT Psalm 2) in a way that is meant to remind listeners of Jewish Jerusalem's initial, crucifixion-provoking hostility toward Jesus and his message.

BCP 1728, Psalm 2:1–2
Why do the <u>heathen</u> so furiously rage together: and why do the people imagine a vain thing? The kings of the earth <u>stand</u> up, and the rulers take counsel together: against the Lord, and against his Anointed.

OT Psalm 2:1–2
Why do [*KJV marginal note:* "Acts 4:25"] the <u>heathen</u> rage, <u>and the</u> people imagine a vain thing? The kings of the earth <u>set themselves</u>, and the rulers take counsel together, against the Lᴏʀᴅ, and against his anointed, **saying,**

Hammond 1659 Psalm 2:1–2
Why do the <u>heathen</u> [*margin*, "nations"] rage [*margin*, "<u>conspire</u>, <u>assemble</u>"], <u>and the</u> people imagine a vain thing? The kings of the earth <u>set themselves</u> [*margin*, "rise up"], and the rulers take counsel [*margin*, "<u>assemble</u>"] together against the Lᴏʀᴅ and against his anointed, **saying,**

NT Acts 4:24–28
Thou art God, . . . who by the mouth of thy servant David hast said [i.e., King David, who prophesied, at OT Psalm 2:1–2], Why did the heathen [i.e., the pagan gentiles] rage, and the people imagine vain things? The kings of the earth stood up, and the rulers were gathered together against the Lord, and against his Christ. For of a truth against thy holy child Jesus, whom thou hast anointed, both

Herod and Pontius Pilate, with the Gentiles, and the people of Israel [i.e., "the Jews"] were gathered together, for to do whatsoever thy hand and thy counsel determined before to be done.

(See also NT Revelation 11:18
And the nations were angry [i.e., as the nations raged, God, against your messiah], and thy wrath is come . . .)

[41] Chorus

Let us break their Bonds asunder, and cast away their Yokes from us.

Psalm 2:3

Paraphrase

[The kings and rulers exclaim:] "Let's break apart their [Jesus and the Lord God's] restraints, and let's reject their yokes.

Notes:

1. In traditional Christian understanding of the time, "their bonds" means the restraints of the Lord God and of God's messiah, Jesus. The bonds and yokes may be understood to be the obligation to obey God that results from the acknowledgment of God as supreme master and Lord. A Christian implication here is that those Jewish people who do not, or refuse to, acknowledge Jesus as Lord are actually rebelling against their obligation to God, who sent Jesus—that is to say, Jews who don't believe in Jesus are flouting the yoke of obedience and the bond of recognizing God's sovereignty.

2. The kings and rulers exclaim this here even though the yoke of God's messiah, Jesus, was earlier lauded as being "easy" (at the libretto's no. 21, above—presumably Jennens adopts Hammond's suggested alternative of

yokes for the BCP and KJV's *cords* to effect this connection between the libretto's nos. 21 and 41).

BCP 1728, Psalm 2:3
Let us break their bonds asunder: and cast away their <u>cords</u> from us.

OT Psalm 2:3
Let us break their <u>bands</u> asunder, and cast away their <u>cords</u> from us.

Hammond 1659, Psalm 2:3
Let us break their bonds asunder, and cast away their <u>cords</u> [*marginal note:* "*or* yokes"] from us.

VII.
[42] Recit

He that dwelleth in Heaven shall laugh them to scorn; the Lord shall have them in Derision.

Psalm 2:4

Paraphrase

He [the resurrected Jesus] who dwells in heaven [sitting at the right hand of God] will laugh them [those rejecting him] to scorn: the Lord Jesus Christ will mock them.

Note:

Earlier—at the libretto's no. 27—*they* ("the Jews") will laugh *him* (Jesus) to scorn; but here *he*, resurrected, in heaven, will laugh *them* ("the Jews," as well as others) to scorn. The Lord's scorn involves, in part, his taking vengeance on Old Israel, above all by destroying its Temple—in any event, by heaping some serious ruin or other on the people of Israel (which is the meaning of OT Psalm 2:1–2 and verse 9, as governed by the use of Psalm 2 at NT Acts 4:25–27; the Lord's vengeance is part of the subject matter for the next several numbers in *Messiah*).

BCP 1728, Psalm 2:4
He that dwelleth in heaven shall laugh them to scorn: the Lord shall have them in derision.

OT Psalm 2:4
He that sitteth in the heavens shall laugh: the LORD shall have them in derision.

(See NT Matthew 27:39–40 and OT Psalm 22:7 at the libretto's recitative no. 27, above.)

[43] Song, *or* Recit

Thou shalt break them with a Rod of Iron; Thou shalt dash them in Pieces like a Potter's Vessel.

Psalm 2:9 → Revelation 2:27–28; 12:5; 19:15

Paraphrase

[Says God to the Lord Jesus Christ:] "You [my messiah, Jesus] will break them [first and emblematically, those Jews who do not accept you as my messiah; and then also the heathen] with an iron rod; you will dash them in pieces like earthenware."

Note:

In traditional Christian understandings (and emphasized, e.g., by Luther), OT Psalm 2 was often taken to mean that God's messiah will "break"

Jews who don't believe in Jesus (especially by destroying Jerusalem and its Temple); and he particularly "dashes" the Old Israelites "in pieces" by scattering them over the earth, far and wide, into a diaspora with no home country to possibly return to. The punishment of "the Jews" is believed to be emblematic of the eventual destruction of God's other "enemies," the heathen. In any case, God is expected to heap some serious ruin or other on the people of Israel (this is part of the meaning of OT Psalm 2:1–2 and verse 9, as governed by the way Psalm 2 is used at NT Acts 4:25–27).

Broader Note:

In the next movement, the extraordinarily exultant Hallelujah chorus, which rejoices over the destruction of God's "enemies" (first and emblematically, over the destruction of Judaism, as explained in the previous note), Handel apparently includes melodic snippets from the Lutheran hymns "Wachet auf, ruft uns die Stimme" and "Wie schön leuchtet der Morgenstern" (*Morgenstern* is the German equivalent of "morning star"—see the citing of NT Revelation 2:27–28 here, two paragraphs up from the set-off text of the next movement in the libretto, no. 44, below). Both of these hymns relate to the story in NT Matthew 25 of the Wise and Foolish Virgins preparing for attendance of the wedding feast of the great bridegroom (see also NT Revelation 19:7–9).

The Matthew 25 story has sometimes, including in Handel's day (and in our day), been understood as a tale of Jesus'—that is, God's—categorical rejection of Synagoga (Judaism) in favor of Ecclesia (Christianity). In the Hallelujah chorus the Christian Church rejoices, in significant part, it appears, over the destruction of Jerusalem and its Temple.

To be altogether clear on the issue of Christianity's "enemies," one might reasonably wonder, If Handel's *Messiah* indeed expresses any triumphal Christian rejoicing against Judaism, doesn't it project the very same attitude correspondingly toward all populations who don't believe in Jesus? Can and should *Messiah*'s anti-Judaism be understood, within this perspective, as a *special* problem?

The answer is yes. Historically, Christian triumphing over Judaism has played out rather differently from its triumphing over paganism, Islam, and other cultural-religious traditions. Notably, Christians' violence against Jews—to cite only several examples: the eleventh-century First Crusade, the fifteenth-century expulsion from Spain, and the extensive direct and indirect complicity in the twentieth-century murder of millions—was against civilians. The pagans, Muslims, and others—like Christians but *not* Jews after the first century CE—typically had armies.

Apparently less well known (or perhaps ignored), however, and well worth calling attention to, is the fact that for Jennens's intended Christian audience (and therefore for any historically informed study of *Messiah*), there is another reason why Christian rejoicing against Judaism has to be understood as a special problem: such rejoicing is contrary to the spirit—and in all probability to the letter—of a (highly specific) directive of the NT. At Romans 11:17–18, the apostle Paul writes: "But if some of the branches were broken [on the cultivated olive tree, a metaphor for the family of God, with the *broken* branches representing those Jews among Israel who do not believe in Jesus] and you [gentile follower of Jesus], being a [shoot from a] wild olive tree, were grafted in among them and became a joint sharer of the root of the richness of the [cultivated] olive tree [i.e., such that the broken but protectively 'callused' branches are still drawing nourishment from the root], *do not rejoice/self-boast against the branches*."

The key word here is *katakauchō*. Biblical-Greek dictionaries define the word as "to boast in triumphant comparison with others," "to glory against," "to exult over," "to boast one's self to the injury of," and "to rejoice against." *Katakauchō* is used also at NT James 2:13b, which the KJV gives as: "mercy *rejoiceth against* judgment."

While the NT often projects a remarkably strong and deep severity toward Jews who do not believe in Jesus (see, e.g., John 8:23–47), there are no scriptural texts that counter Romans 11 by suggesting that Christian schadenfreude against Judaism is ever fitting. Of course, the Psalms are revered as part of Christian Scripture, and many of the Psalms rejoice in the destruction of the enemies of God's covenant people. But if one determines from this that it's therefore biblically right or fitting for Christians to re-joice against Judaism, then he or she presumes, against Romans 9–11, that Jews are not biblically God's covenant people. The belief that post-Jesus Jews are not God's people has fueled much Christian anti-Jewish sentiment and violent action.

Whether or not one accepts that, in *Messiah*, Psalm 2 is to be under-stood in part as prefiguring specifically the destruction of Jerusalem and its Temple, the Hallelujah chorus is nevertheless undeniably a joyous ut-terance following directly upon movements that speak, in significant part, of some fierce ruin or another for "the people [of Israel]." (See Psalm 2:9 and 2:1, which, for *Messiah,* are to be read typologically in light of the NT glossing of Psalm 2:1 at Acts 4:25–29, where Psalm 2's "the people" is spe-cifically identified as Jesus-threatening ethnic Israel—and thus the words "of Israel" are supposed to be read into Jennens's libretto.)

If a chorus gives expression to *any* joy or gratitude right after the li-bretto's reference to the dashing to pieces of a "them" that includes Jews, then that choral number—whether intentionally or not, and whether natu-rally picked up and endorsed by listeners or not—is effectively disobey-ing Paul's instruction for Christians not to rejoice and/or self-boast against Judaism.

Given that the particular biblical, theological, and historical relation-ships of the Christian Church to Jewish unbelievers in Jesus are fundamen-tally different from those of the church to gentile unbelievers, the very act of rejoicing in any form by New Israel over any sort of ruin experienced by so-called Old Israel inherently and essentially involves a kind of self-exaltation. This entails the vaunting of assumed superiority by a mere grafted shoot from a wild olive tree over and against the natural branches from the cultivated olive tree, even if the joy expressed does not feature verbally explicit self-boasting.

BCP 1728, Psalm 2:9
Thou shalt <u>bruise</u> them with a rod of iron: <u>and break</u> them in pieces like a potter's vessel.

OT Psalm 2:9

Thou shalt break them with a rod of iron; thou shalt dash them in
pieces like a potter's vessel.

NT Revelation 12:5

And she [i.e., the woman of Revelation 12:1 (typically interpreted,
in Protestant readings, to represent Ecclesia, Christianity) clothed
with the sun (typically interpreted to represent the righteousness of
Jesus), and the moon (typically interpreted to represent the feeble
light of the Law of Moses, kept by Synagoga, Judaism), under her
feet, and upon her head a crown of twelve stars (typically interpreted to represent the gospel of Jesus, which is preached by his
apostles, "the Twelve")] brought forth a man-child [i.e., who is typically interpreted to represent the family of saints that are the members of the "body of Christ," those who belong to the church] who
was to rule all nations [i.e., typically interpreted as "the Christian
Church was to rule all nations—Jewish and gentile, with Jesus as
king"] with a rod of iron: and her child was caught up unto God,
and to his throne [i.e., the family of saints ascended into heaven,
just like Jesus].

NT Revelation 2:27–28

And he [i.e., the disciple of Jesus, who overcomes, and keeps the
Son of God's works to the end] shall rule them [i.e., the unbelieving
nations—Jewish and gentile] with a rod of iron: as the vessels of
a potter shall they be broken to shivers) even as I [i.e., the Son of
God, Jesus] received of my Father. And I [i.e., Jesus] will give him
[i.e., that persevering victorious disciple] the morning star [i.e., I
will give the persevering victorious disciple my Self].

NT Revelation 19:15

And out of his [i.e., from Christ's, the Word of God's] mouth goeth
a sharp sword, that with it he should smite the nations [i.e., unbelievers among the gentiles and Jews]: and he shall rule them with

a rod of iron: and he treadeth the wine-press of the fierceness and wrath of almighty God.

VIII.

[44] Chorus

Hallelujah! for the Lord God Omnipotent reigneth.

Revelation 19:6

Paraphrase

Hallelujah—praise be to God!, because the all-powerful Lord God reigns.

Notes:

1. At the notes on the libretto's no. 43, above, see the broader note discussing the juxtaposition of this rejoicing chorus to the previous number's predicting of violence first and emblematically against "the Jews."

2. *Hallelujah* means "praise be to God." Hebrew: *Hallelu*—"Let us praise"; *Jah*, or *Yah*, means "God."

3. Here we are meant to know that the Lord God reigns from God's bringing about the downfall of the unbelievers in Jesus, who sin in rejecting God's messiah.

NT Revelation 19:6

And I heard as it were the voice of a great multitude, and as the voice of many waters, and as the voice of mighty thunderings, saying, <u>Alleluia</u>: for the Lord God omnipotent reigneth.

Wells, Revelation 19:6

Hallelujah; for the Lord God omnipotent reigneth.

[44] Chorus, *continued*

---

*The Kingdom of this World is become the Kingdom of our Lord and of his
    Christ; and He shall reign for ever and ever,*

Revelation 11:15 ← Exodus 15:18

Paraphrase

*The kingdom of this world has become the kingdom of our Lord
God, and of the Christ, God's messiah, Jesus; and he [God's messiah,
the "King of Kings, and Lord of Lords"] will reign for ever and ever.*

Note:

The word *Christ* comes from the NT Greek word *christos*, rendering the
OT Hebrew word *mashiyach*—"messiah."

NT Revelation 11:15

And the seventh angel sounded [the trumpet], **and there were great
voices in heaven, saying,** The <u>kingdoms</u> of this world <u>are</u> become
the <u>kingdoms</u> of our Lord, and of his Christ, and he shall reign for
ever and ever.

(See also the Greek source for KJV, Revelation 11:15
. . . *basileiai tou kosmou* . . . ["kingdoms of this world"].)

Wells, Revelation 11:15

The kingdom of this world is become the kingdom of our Lord, and
of his Christ, and he shall reign for ever and ever.

(See also the Greek source for *Wells*, Revelation 11:15
. . . *basileia tou kosmou* . . . ["kingdom of this world"].)

(See also *Vulgate* Revelation 11:15
. . . *regnum huius mundi* . . . ["kingdom of this world"].)

OT Exodus 15:18
The LORD shall reign for ever and ever.

[44] Chorus, *further continued*

King of Kings, and Lord of Lords.

Revelation 19:16

Hallelujah!

(Revelation 19:6)

Paraphrase

[Jesus Christ is the] greatest of kings, and greatest of lords.
Hallelujah—*praise be to God!*

NT Revelation 19:16
And he [i.e., the Word of God, Christ] **hath on his vesture and on
his thigh a name written,** KING OF KINGS, AND LORD OF LORDS.

NT 1 Timothy 6:15
. . . [our Lord Jesus Christ] **who is the blessed and only Potentate,
the** King of kings, and Lord of lords;

(See also NT Revelation 1:5
. . . Jesus Christ, who is . . . the prince of the kings of the earth. . . .)

(See also NT Revelation 17:14
He [i.e., the Lamb: Christ] is Lord of lords, and King of kings . . .)

PART THREE

I.

[45] Song

---

*I know that my Redeemer liveth, and that He shall stand at the latter Day
    upon the Earth:*
And tho' Worms destroy this Body, yet in my Flesh shall I see God.

Job 19:25–26

Paraphrase

*I know that my Redeemer [Jesus] lives, and that at the Last Day [the
"Day of Judgment"] he will stand on the earth [to summon the dead
out of their graves]. And though worms will destroy this, my* earthly
body, *nonetheless with my own eyes [from my transformed,* heavenly
body] *will I see God.*

Notes:

1. In traditional Christian understandings, "my Redeemer" is God's
messiah, Jesus.

2. NT 1 Corinthians 15:35–55 conveys the apostle Paul's understanding of an earthly body's being resurrected as a *transformed*, heavenly body.
His understanding is quite different from two views prevalent among
Christians today: many believe that in heaven they will simply regain their
earthly bodies (as reconstituted and reanimated by God); some others believe that it is only on earth that they have a tangible, solid body, whereas
in heaven they will live eternally as a *disembodied* spirit or soul (a notion
blatantly at odds with the concluding affirmations of the Apostles' Creed,
"I believe . . . in the resurrection of the body, and the life everlasting").

For Paul, "resurrection of the dead" means not resuscitation but transformation of the body. And so there is both a continuity and a discontinuity between what he calls the "psychical body" (Greek, *sōma psychikon*) of the present life and the "pneumatic body" (*sōma pneumatikon*) of the afterlife, somewhat analogous to the continuity and discontinuity between the sown seed and the grown plant: the two look different, but we of course realize that the plant arises from the seed. (And in Greco-Roman biology, further, it was believed that plant seeds and human seeds contained fully formed embryos, as is assumed for NT 1 Corinthians 15:38.) The natural, earthly body (*sōma psychikon*) is animated by the human soul (*psychē*); but the ("saved") spiritual, heavenly body (*sōma pneumatikon*) is animated by the spirit (*pneuma*) of God and is therefore not subject to decay.

Paul further, it seems, made a critical distinction between "flesh" (Greek, *sarx*) and "the body" (*sōma*), one that was not recognized in much later traditional Christian teaching (where theologians often failed to delineate clearly a distinction between *sarx* and *sōma*, such that the former is a constituent of the latter). Having written at 1 Corinthians 15:44, "The body [*sōma*] is sown a psychical body; it is raised a pneumatic body," Paul then, at verse 50, goes on to declare that "flesh [*sarx*] and blood cannot inherit the kingdom of God." Being of the (worldly) sphere of sin's operations, *sarx* must die altogether. Indeed, at the Last Day, *pneuma* can be "saved," but *sarx* is "ruined" (1 Corinthians 5:5).

In the ancient world, "flesh and blood" were often understood not as the whole body but as only a part of the material stuff of the body. Paul, then, holds the particular view that the earthly human body (what he calls the *sōma psychikon*) is made up of *sarx*, *psychē*, and *pneuma*, all three of them being for him what we today would call "physical" or "material." Paul's letter is often misunderstood today, because his terms *psychē* and *pneuma*—in English, typically rendered as "soul" and "spirit"—readily, but altogether mistakenly, suggest noncorporeality to readers who don't know the biblical-historical background. Platonism teaches that "spirit" is an altogether different order of being, one that is, unlike the body, completely nonmaterial. Paul, however, was not a Platonist.

In short, according to Paul, a transformed, heavenly body—the *soma pneumatikon*—is stripped of the corruptible material stuff of *sarx* and *psychē* but retains from the earthly body the immortal material stuff of *pneuma*.

3. The Hebrew source word *basar* (KJV, "flesh") is often rendered as *sarx* in the Septuagint. Here at Job 19:26, however, the Septuagint renders the Hebrew *basar* with the Greek word *derma* (i.e., "skin"—see also NT Hebrews 11:37 and Mark 1:6). For *sarx* as the underlying source word in biblical texts employed in *Messiah*, see OT Isaiah 40:5 (libretto, no. 4); NT Acts 2:31 (no. 32), 1 Corinthians 15:50 (see also no. 47), Luke 3:6 (no. 4), and 1 Timothy 3:16 (Jennens's epigraph).

Broader Note:

The Hebrew text of OT Job 19:25–26 with its extraordinary poetic difficulties is virtually untranslatable; and so, the KJV and BCP renderings owe a great deal of their (possibly false) linguistic clarity to NT teachings about death.

In the Hebrew of Job 19 there is no explicit mention of a "day," or of "worms," or of a "body"; also, the phrase "in my flesh" should arguably be "without my flesh."

Compare then, for example, these three prominent current translations: (1) The New International Version reads, with its footnoted alternatives given here in square brackets, "I know that my Redeemer [or, 'defender'] lives, and that in the end he will stand upon the earth [or, 'upon my grave']. And after my skin has been destroyed, yet [or, 'And after I awake, though this body has been destroyed, then'] in [or, 'apart from'] my flesh I will see God." (2) Young's Literal Translation reads, "That—I have known my Redeemer, the Living and the Last, for the dust he doth rise. And after my skin hath compassed this, then from my flesh I see God." And (3) the Jewish Publication Society Tanakh reads, "But I know that my Vindicator lives; in the end He will testify on earth—this, after my skin will have been peeled off. But I would behold God while still in my flesh."

BCP 1728, *Burial Service*
I know that my Redeemer liveth, and that he shall stand at the latter day upon the earth. And though **after my skin,** worms destroy
this body; yet in my flesh shall I see God . . .

OT Job 19:25–26
For I know that my redeemer liveth, and that he shall stand at the
latter day upon the earth. And though **after my skin,** worms destroy
this body, yet in my flesh shall I see God . . . [*KJV marginal note:*
"*Or,* After I shall awake, though this body be destroyed, yet out of
my flesh shall I see God."]

(See also NT Luke 2:26,29–30
And it was revealed unto him [i.e., to Simeon] by the holy Ghost,
that he should not see death before he had seen the Lord's
Christ. . . . Lord, now lettest thou thy servant [i.e., me, Simeon]
depart in peace, according to thy word. For mine eyes have seen thy
salvation.)

(See also NT John 6:40
And this is the will of him [i.e., God] that sent me [i.e., Jesus], that
every one which seeth the Son [i.e., Jesus], and believeth on him,
may have everlasting life: and I [i.e., Jesus] will raise him up at the
last day.)

(See also NT 1 Corinthians 15:44
It [i.e., the resurrection of the dead] is sown a natural body; it is
raised a spiritual body. There is a natural body [i.e., the *earthly*
body, which is *animated by the human soul* (biblical Greek: by
the "psyche")], and there is a spiritual body [i.e., the transformed,
heavenly body, which is a *spiritual* body in that this transformed
body is *animated by God's spirit* and therefore not subject to
decay].)

[45] Song, *continued*

For now is Christ risen from the Dead, the First-Fruits of them that sleep.

1 Corinthians 15:20

Paraphrase

[I know this—namely, that my Redeemer lives] because now Christ is risen from the dead, and he, Jesus, is the "firstfruits" of those who "sleep."

Note:

In the apostle Paul's understanding, Jesus is the "firstfruits" of the "harvest offering" of humanity to God of those who "sleep" in their earthly graves.

In ancient Israel annually on the day after the first Sabbath in Passover the "firstfruits" of the harvest were waved before God (OT Leviticus 23:10–11) as an offering that sanctified the rest of the harvest to come (OT Proverbs 3:9–10); and so Paul writes (at NT 1 Corinthians 15:20) that Jesus' resurrection, taking place on the day after the first Sabbath in Passover, works as "firstfruits," guaranteeing a blessed forthcoming "harvest": the resurrection and blessing of all those who believe in him, God's messiah.

BCP 1728, *Burial Service*
Now is Christ risen from the dead, **and become** the first-fruits of them that slept.

NT 1 Corinthians 15:20
But now is Christ risen from the dead, **and become** the first-fruits of them that slept.

BCP 1638, *Burial Service*
Christ is risen from the dead, **and become** the first-fruits of them
that sleep.

Wells, 1 Corinthians 15:20
But now is Christ risen from the dead, the first-fruits of them
that slept.

[46] Chorus

Since by Man came Death, by Man came also the Resurrection of the Dead.
For as in Adam *all die, even so in* Christ *shall all be made alive.*

1 Corinthians 15:21–22 ← [Daniel 12:2]

Paraphrase

Since death came by a human, the resurrection of the dead also came
by a human. Because as in the man Adam all die, just so in the man
Jesus Christ will all be made alive.

Notes:

1. Death came through the first man, Adam (Hebrew: *adam*, "man"),
the old "adam," who per se disobeyed God, in the Garden of Eden (OT
Genesis 3), and thus brought sickness and death into the world.

2. Resurrection of the dead came through the new "adam," Christ Jesus,
who per se obeyed God, to the point of dying on the cross.

3. In traditional Christian understandings, all humanity—believers and
unbelievers—will be "made alive" (i.e., resurrected) to face Jesus Christ's
judgment; only believers in Jesus, however, will be "saved," to heavenly
"eternal life."

BCP 1728, *Burial Service* / NT 1728 1 Corinthians 15:21–22
For since by man came death, by man came also the resurrection of
the dead. For as in Adam all die, even so in Christ shall all be made
alive.

(See also OT Daniel 12:2
And many of them that sleep in the dust of the earth shall awake
["spiritually," or perhaps bodily], some to everlasting life, and some
to shame and everlasting contempt.)

II.

[47] Recit accomp

Behold, I tell you a Mystery: We shall not all sleep, but we shall all be
changed, in a Moment, in the Twinkling of an Eye, at the last Trumpet.

1 Corinthians 15:51–52a

Paraphrase

*Look, I [the apostle, Paul] am speaking to you [believers in Jesus
Christ] of a mystery: not all of us [believers] will "sleep" [in our
graves, that is to say, not all of us will die before the Second Coming of Christ]; all of us [followers of Christ—not only those of us
who have already died, but also those of us who will still be alive at
the time that Christ comes back, to judge the living and the dead],
however, will be changed [such that the present earthly body will
be* transformed *into a heavenly body, animated by God's spirit and
therefore not subject to decay]; this will happen in a flash, in the
twinkling of an eye—at the "last trumpet" [whose sound announces
the Day of Judgment].*

BCP 1728, *Burial Service* / NT 1728 1 Corinthians 15:50–52a
Now this I [the apostle Paul] **say, brethren** [i.e., you fellow believers in Jesus Christ], **that** [earthly] **flesh and blood cannot inherit the kingdom of God; neither doth corruption inherit incorruption.**
Behold, I <u>shew</u> you a mystery; We [i.e., we believers in Jesus Christ] shall not all sleep, but we shall all be changed, in a moment, in the twinkling of an eye, at the last <u>trump,</u>

Wells, 1 Corinthians 15:51–52a
Behold, I tell you a mystery: We [i.e., we believers in Jesus Christ] shall not all sleep, but we [i.e., we believers in Jesus Christ] shall all be changed, in a moment, in the twinkling of an eye, at the last trumpet;

[48] Song

The Trumpet shall sound, and the Dead shall be raised incorruptible, and
  We shall be changed.
For this Corruptible must put on Incorruption, and this Mortal must put
  on Immortality. [DA CAPO.]

1 Corinthians 15:52b–53 ← [Joel 2:1]

Paraphrase

The trumpet will sound [announcing the Day of Judgment] and the dead [believers] will be resurrected such that they [that is, their bodies] will not decay, and we [the believers in Christ who are still alive on earth at the Second Coming of Jesus] will be transformed. This will be so, because this [body] that decays [the "natural body" of the follower of Jesus] must be clothed [with God's spirit] so that it [the

transformed, "spiritual body"] will not decay, and this mortal [body
of the believer in Christ] must be clothed with what is immortal.

Note:

In the traditional understanding of the NT, dead believers in Jesus Christ
will be made alive again at the Second Coming of Christ with transformed,
non-decaying heavenly bodies; and the earthly bodies of the then still-living
believers will be transformed instantaneously, without dying first, into having heavenly, non-decaying bodies.

The resurrected body of the unbeliever in Jesus, however, is not described; unbelievers in Jesus will be condemned and, according to NT Revelation 20:7–15, be "cast into the lake of fire"; indeed, such unbelievers
are considered, according to NT John 3:18, even now, in the present life,
"already condemned," because they have "not believed in the name of the
only begotten Son of God," Jesus.

NT 1728 1 Corinthians 15:52b–53
for the trumpet shall sound and the dead shall be raised incorruptible, and we [i.e., we believers in Jesus Christ] shall be changed. For
this corruptible must put on incorruption, and this mortal must put
on immortality.

BCP 1728, *Burial Service*
(**for** the trumpet shall sound, and the dead shall be raised incorruptible, and we [i.e., we believers in Jesus Christ] shall be changed.)
For this corruptible must put on incorruption, and this mortal must
put on immortality.

(See also OT Joel 2:1
Blow ye the trumpet in Zion, and sound an alarm in my holy
mountain: let all the inhabitants of the land tremble: for the day of
the LORD cometh, for it is nigh at hand.)

III.

[49] Recit

Then shall be brought to pass the Saying that is written; Death is swallow'd up in Victory.

1 Corinthians 15:54 ← Isaiah 25:8

Paraphrase

Then [and not before then] will be brought to fulfillment the saying that is written, "Death is utterly destroyed in [Jesus'] victory."

Note:

The "*saying* that is written" is OT Isaiah 25:8.

BCP 1728, *Burial Service* / NT 1728 1 Corinthians 15:54
So when this corruptible shall have put on incorruption, and this mortal shall have put on immortality, then shall be brought to pass the saying that is written, Death is swallowed up in victory.

OT Isaiah 25:8
He [i.e., the Lord God of hosts] will swallow up death in victory . . .

(See also *Greek Septuagint*, Isaiah 25:8
Death has prevailed and swallowed men up . . .)

(See also *Hebrew Text*, Isaiah 25:8
He will swallow death forever . . .)

(See also *Theodotion*, Isaiah 25:8
Death is swallowed up in victory . . .)

[50] Duet (or Recit?)[8]

O Death, where is thy Sting? O Grave, where is thy Victory?
The Sting of Death is Sin, and the Strength of Sin is the Law.

1 Corinthians 15:55–56 ← Hosea 13:14

Paraphrase

O death, where now is your poison-stinger? O grave, Hades, where is your victory? Death's poison-stinger is sin, and sin's power [the power to increase guilt] is in the Law.

BCP 1728, *Burial Service* / NT 1728 1 Corinthians 15:55–56
O death, where is thy sting? O grave, where is thy victory? The sting of death is sin; and the strength of sin is the law.

(See also the Greek source for KJV, 1 Corinthians 15:55–56
. . . *pou sou thanatē to kentron, pou sou adē to nikos* . . . ["Where, death, is your sting? Where, Hades, is your victory?"].)

OT Hosea 13:14
O death, I [i.e., the Lord your God] will be thy plagues; O grave, I will be thy destruction . . .

(See also *Hebrew Text*, Hosea 13:14
O death, where are thy plagues; O Sheol, where is thy destruction . . .)

(See also *Greek Septuagint*, Hosea 13:14
O death, where is thy punishment; O Hades, where is thy sting . . .)

[51] Chorus

But Thanks be to God, who giveth Us the Victory through our Lord Jesus Christ.

1 Corinthians 15:57

Paraphrase

But thanks be to God, who gives us the victory [over sin and death] through our Lord Jesus Christ.

Notes:

1. In traditional understandings, the "victory," through Jesus, is over sin and death.

2. *We*, the followers of the gospel of Jesus, God's messiah, receive the victory, and not, for example, those who cleave to the (now obsolete) Law of Moses.

3. Several modern commentators have bizarrely claimed that Handel's oratorio never mentions God's messiah by name. The chorus here at the libretto's no. 51, however, exclaims the name *Jesus* at bars 7, 10, 12, 29, 37, and 46, as well as in a drawn-out cadence at the close, bar 49.

BCP 1728, *Burial Service* / NT 1728 1 Corinthians 15:57
But thanks be to God, <u>which</u> giveth us the victory, through our Lord Jesus Christ.

Wells, 1 Corinthians 15:57
But thanks be to God, who giveth us the victory <u>thro'</u> our Lord Jesus Christ.

Deacon 1734, *Burial Service*
But thanks be to God, who giveth us the victory through our Lord
Jesus Christ.

[52] Song

If God be [Handel's setting: or, *is*] *for us, who can be against us?*

Romans 8:31 ← [Psalm 118:6]

Paraphrase

If God is for us [*believers in Christ Jesus*], *if God is on our side, who
can be* [*successful in efforts*] *against us?*

NT Romans 8:31
What shall we then say to these things? If God be for us, who can
be against us?

(See also *Luther Bible*, Romans 8:31
Ist Gott für uns, wer mag wieder uns sein? ["If God is for us, who
may be against us?"].)

(See also OT Psalm 118:6
The Lord is on my side; I will not fear: what can man do
unto me?)

[52] Song, *continued*

Who shall lay any thing to the Charge of God's Elect?
It is God that justifieth; who is he that condemneth?

It is Christ that died, yea, rather that is risen again; who is at the Right-Hand of God; who maketh [Handel's setting, sometimes: *makes*] *Intercession for us.*

Romans 8:33–34 ← Isaiah 50:8–9a, Psalm 110:1

Paraphrase

Who will be [successful in] bringing any charge against them who are God's chosen ones [against them who are called by God to saving faith in Christ Jesus]? [No one, since] the Lord God is the one that justifies [for salvation those that God calls to faith in Jesus]; but who is the one that condemns? Christ is the one that died, yes indeed—rather, it is Christ that is risen again [from the dead]—who is [in heaven] at the right hand of God; yes, it is Jesus Christ who makes intercession with God for us [Christ does not condemn us; that is, he doesn't condemn us Christians, God's chosen ones].

Note:

The text can't be saying that no one will ever bring a charge against the elect—at the very least, Satan is the accuser. Rather, it must be saying that no one will succeed in such an effort, since God is on the side of the elect.

NT Romans 8:33–34
Who shall lay any thing to the charge of God's elect? It is God that justifieth: who is he that condemneth? It is Christ that died, yea, rather that is risen again, who is **even** at the right hand of God, who **also** maketh intercession for us.

OT Isaiah 50:8–9a
He is near that justifieth me; who will contend with me? . . . Behold, the Lord GOD will help me; who is he that shall condemn me?

OT Psalm 110:1

The LORD said unto my Lord, Sit thou at my right hand, until I make thine enemies my footstool.

IV.

[53] Chorus

Worthy is the Lamb that was slain, and hath redeemed us to God by his Blood, to receive Power, and Riches, and Wisdom, and Strength, and Honour, and Glory, and Blessing.

Blessing, and Honour, and Glory, and Power, be unto Him [Handel's setting: Blessing and honour, glory and power be unto him] that sitteth upon the Throne, and unto the Lamb, for ever and ever.

Revelation 5:9,12–13

Paraphrase

The Lamb of God, Jesus, who was slain on the cross, and who has redeemed us [the Christian Church] to God by Jesus' blood is worthy to receive power, and riches, and wisdom, and strength, and honor, and glory, and blessing. Blessing and honor, glory and power be to God sitting on the throne in heaven, and to the Lamb, Jesus Christ, God the Son [whom we worship with "new song" and who sits at the right hand of God], for ever and ever.

NT Revelation 5:9,12–13

And they sung a new song, saying, Thou art worthy to take the book, and to open the seals thereof: for thou wast slain, and <u>hast</u> redeemed us to God by <u>thy</u> blood **out of every kindred, and tongue, and people, and nation; . . . Saying with a loud voice, Worthy is the** Lamb that was slain, to receive power, and riches, and wisdom, and strength, and honour, and glory, and blessing. **And every creature which is in heaven, and on the earth, and under the earth, and such as are in the sea, and all that are in them, heard I, saying,** Blessing, and honour, **and** glory, and power, be unto him that sitteth upon the throne, and unto the Lamb for ever and ever.

(See also OT Exodus 12:1–27 and Isaiah 53:7a.)

Deacon 1734, *"The Morning Hymn"*
Worthy is the Lamb that was slain, to receive power, and riches, and wisdom, and strength, and honour, and glory, and blessing; <u>for he</u> hath redeemed us to God by his blood, **out of every kindred, and tongue, and people, and nation. Therefore** blessing, honour, glory, and power, be unto him that sitteth <u>on</u> the throne, and unto the Lamb, for ever and ever. Amen. **(Hallelujah.)**

[54] Chorus

Amen.

(Revelation 5:14, 22:20b–21)

Amen.

Note:

The (Hebrew) word *amen* means "so be it," or "this is the truth." *Amen* appears at Revelation 5:14, and then again at 22:21 as the last word in the Christian Bible.

NT Revelation 5:14
And the four beasts said, Amen. And the four and twenty elders fell down and worshipped him that liveth for ever and ever.

NT Revelation 22:20b–21

Come Lord Jesus. The grace of our Lord Jesus Christ be with you all. Amen.

(See also OT Malachi 4:6

Behold, I [i.e., God] will send you [i.e., send to you, my messiah-expecting people] Elijah the prophet [i.e., I will send you John the Baptist, the Elijah-figure who will announce the appearance of my messiah, Jesus] before the coming of the great and dreadful day of the LORD. And he [i.e., John the Baptist] shall turn the heart of the fathers to the children, and the heart of the children to their fathers, lest I [i.e., God] come and smite the earth with a curse [i.e., for people's not believing in my messiah, Jesus; this is the way the (Protestant) OT ends, with a curse, whereas the NT ends with a blessing; note, then, that because the curse in Malachi 4:6 is also a prediction about the coming of "Elijah," an ending of the OT with the book of Malachi serves as a segue to the Gospel narratives, through John the Baptist, a bridge figure seen as simultaneously the last of the OT-style prophets and the first of the NT figures; note too, then, that the Jewish Bible gives its books in a different ordering: it ends not with the book of Malachi but with the book of 2 Chronicles].)

NOTES

I. INTRODUCTION

1. "Unsettling History of That Joyous 'Hallelujah,'" *New York Times*, Sunday Arts & Leisure, April 8, 2007; reprinted in *International Herald Tribune* (Paris), Culture, April 24, 2007.

2. Arthur Danto, "The Space of Beauty," *New Republic* (1982), quoted in Richard Eldridge, *An Introduction to the Philosophy of Art* (2003).

3. Throughout, to avoid appearing to endorse the notion of ascribing a collective will to Jews, I place the expression "the Jews" in quotation marks; see Berel Lang's remarkably astute essay "On the 'the' in 'the Jews,'" *Midstream* (2003).

4. Such thinking is proclaimed even at the highest ecclesiastical levels, serving as inspiration for ensuing sermons; see, e.g., John Bluck, *The Giveaway God: Ecumenical Bible Studies on Divine Generosity* (2001), discussed in Amy-Jill Levine, *The Misunderstood Jew: The Church and the Scandal of the Jewish Jesus* (2006). (Bluck, an Anglican priest, was the communications director for the World Council of Churches.)

5. One couldn't in fact rightly say that this aspect of *Messiah* went unnoticed until now. Vigorous theological anti-Judaism figures prominently, and altogether approvingly, in the first book published on this oratorio: John Newton's *Messiah: Fifty Expository Discourses, on the Series of Scriptural Passages, which form the Subject of the Celebrated Oratorio of Handel* (1786). It features also to some extent in the musical discussion of *Messiah* in Charles Burney's book *An Account of the Musical Performances in Westminster-Abbey, and the Pantheon . . . 1784: In Commemoration of Handel* (1785).

6. Among the unpublished portion of the correspondence with his friend the Virgil scholar Edward Holdsworth (Jennens-Holdsworth

correspondence, 1729–46, the original manuscripts of which are now housed at the Foundling Museum in London), I've made another discovery that shows Jennens's detailed knowledge of Hammond. In a letter marked "Gops[all]. May 14. 1742.," Jennens writes to Holdsworth: "If I remember right, D^r. Hammond [at Acts 16:12] translates τῆς μερίδος as you do, *a part* or *one part*." Hammond's New Testament commentary does indeed suggest that the King James reading of Acts 16:12, "[from the city of Neapolis we came] to Philippi, which is *the chief* city of *that* part of Macedonia," should be emended as "to Philippi, which is *a prime* city of *a* part of Macedonia."

Further evidence of Jennens's apparent penchant for consulting widely and deeply in his religious reference works is found in a letter of his to Holdsworth headed "Q[ueen]. Square. Feb. 4. 1741–2.," where Jennens refers to "searching [in] my [various biblical] Commentators . . . [including, for example, Jean] Le Clerc & [Sebastian] Castellio."

7. Some of the key material appeared in my academic article "Rejoicing against Judaism in Handel's *Messiah*," *Journal of Musicology* (2007). Leading Handel expert John H. Roberts has published a long and vociferous response, "False *Messiah*," *Journal of the American Musicological Society* (2010). Attentive scholarly readers will see that throughout the course of the present book, without always saying so directly, most of the objections of the Roberts article are addressed. Here I'll make only general observations.

Roberts's article states that in my "tendentious," "forced," and "exaggerated" *Journal of Musicology* article, "ample evidence, prejudicially interpreted, has yielded a result that is demonstrably false." The *JOM* article represented its anti-Judaic readings for *Messiah*, however, as one aspect of the oratorio's meanings, declaring at the outset, "Although rejoicing against Judaism is certainly not the whole story of [*Messiah*], it is a significant and generally unrecognized aspect of the narrative." The *Journal of the American Musicological Society* article, not taking this central qualifying statement into account, reads as though the *JOM* piece had claimed that anti-Judaism was the sole or primary message of *Messiah*. This is a glaring flaw, and the *JAMS* article certainly does not prove that a proposed aspect of a work's meaning is "demonstrably false" by showing that there is "ample evidence" for broader aspects within the work's range of plausible meanings. The projection of anti-Judaic sentiment would have to be *incompatible* with the broader aspects to render the former "false."

Roberts's article actually provides not what it deems "alternative" interpretations but logically complementary ones: they do not render invalid the readings for which the *JOM* article had argued. To say that *Messiah* addresses other contemporary religious concerns, that it was devotional in function, or that it condemns all unbelievers in Jesus does not refute a claim that the work contains significant anti-Judaic sentiment. Roberts's work projects a radical misreading of the *JOM* article's assessing of evidence, and likewise of its reasoning and conclusions.

The philosopher Peter Kivy has likewise published a response, "*Messiah*'s Message: Con or Anti," in his book *Sounding Off: Eleven Essays in the Philosophy of Music* (2012), which takes the *JOM* article to be the work of "the anti-Semitism-hunter" who would place *Messiah* as "the target next [after Bach's *Passions*] in the line of fire." Kivy's essay says that it "make[s] no claim to biblical, historical, musicological, or any other variety of erudition" but, remarkably for an academic book of philosophy, expresses the hope that "by the application of some common sense, some ordinary logic, and some ordinary intuitions about meaning, to shed some light on the issue, and, in so doing, cast some doubt in the direction of Marissen's claim that Handel's *Messiah* evinces [anti-Judaic] sentiments." Along the way, "the charge of [anti-Judaism] advanced by Marissen against our [!] beloved Hallelujah chorus" is absurdly likened to the traitorousness of Brutus's stabbing to death of his friend Julius Caesar.

8. I've adapted this paragraph from the preface in Michael Marissen, *Bach's Oratorios* (2008).

II. REJOICING AGAINST JUDAISM IN HANDEL'S *MESSIAH*

1. For example, Herbert Weinstock, *Handel* (1946): "Pleased and heartened by the [positive] light in which one of their national heroes was being presented to the English public, many Jews hurried to patronize Covent Garden, appreciably swelling the box office for [Handel's oratorio] *Judas Maccabaeus*. Their recruitment helped Handel present that oratorio six times during its first season, thirty-eight times before his death twelve years later. [Thomas] Morell [the librettist] and Handel saw at once the desirability of Jewish patronage at Covent Garden."

2. Scholarly and journalistic biographers have continually trotted out a remark of Handel's that they say proves he received particular support from London's Jewish community. But we don't know for a fact that Handel made the remark, and in any event the remark may strike more judicious readers as not exactly positive toward Jews. The following paragraph from David Hunter's important and widely overlooked or ignored article "George Frideric Handel and the Jews: Fact, Fiction, and the Tolerances of Scholarship" (2002) deserves to be quoted in full: "The only remark of Handel's concerning Jews that has survived comes via librettist Thomas Morell, who wrote in a letter to an unknown recipient, at least fifteen years after the event, that Handel had said that 'the Jews will not come to [hear his oratorio *Theodora*] (as [they will] to [his oratorio] *Judas* [*Maccabaeus*])

because it is a Christian story; and the Ladies will not come, because it [is] a virtuous one.' First published in [the 1780s], the remark makes little sense. Not only does it lay the blame for thin houses on marginalized others, it is illogical in terms of the Jews supporting only Israelite oratorios and women supporting only romantic or salacious ones. The rhetorical device omits the group to which the composer and librettist belong and that ought to be supporting Handel, namely Christian males! Had the remark any logic, then those leaders of society should have been flocking to *Theodora*. If it is an accurate record of Handel's opinion, then the remark is hardly flattering (not surprisingly, biographers have failed to unpack its prejudices). At the very least it is indicative of conventional dismissive attitudes toward Jews and women."

3. As is rightly noted in Ruth Smith, *Handel's Oratorios and Eighteenth-Century Thought* (1995); Smith's magnificent study does not, however, take note or consideration of Kidder's full subtitle and its import.

The list of titles in Jennens's theological library is brilliantly reconstructed in Tassilo Erhardt, *Händels Messiah: Text, Musik, Theologie* (2007).

4. Shortly before Jennens compiled his *Messiah* libretto, an abbreviated version of Kidder's *Demonstration* was also published, as "That Part of Bishop Kidder's Demonstration of the Messias, Preach'd at Boyle's Lectures, Abridg'd," in Gilbert Burnet (Vicar of Coggeshall, not to be confused with the earlier bishop of Salisbury of the same name), ed., *A Defence of Natural and Revealed Religion: Being an Abridgment of the Sermons preached at the Lecture founded by the Honble Robert Boyle, Esq;* (1737). The very first sentence of this abridgement reads: "As the obstinate [religious] Infidelity of the *Jews* is very amazing, I design to make a strict Enquiry into the Causes and Occasions of it."

The Boyle Lectures were founded by the renowned chemist, natural philosopher, and biblical scholar Robert Boyle (1627–91), who in his will (printed, for example, in *The Works of the Honourable Robert Boyle* [1744]) left "an annual salary for some learned divine, or preaching minister . . . who shall be injoined to perform the offices following, *viz.* first to preach eight sermons in the year for proving the Christian Religion against notorious Infidels, *viz.* Atheists, Theists, Pagans, Jews, and Mahometans, [but] not descending lower to any controversies that are [engaged in] among Christians themselves."

5. Typology continues to have significant meaning for many Christians today. The classic text is Ernst Wilhelm Hengstenberg, *Christologie des Alten Testaments und Commentar über die messianischen Weissagungen der Propheten* (1829–35; 2nd ed., 1854–57); trans. by Reuel Kieth: *Christology of the Old Testament, and a Commentary on the Predictions of the*

Messiah by the Prophets (1836–39; trans. of 2nd ed. by Theodore Meyer and James Martin, 1854–65).

Hengstenberg was an anti-rationalist and therefore reflects the exegesis of pre-rationalist biblical commentators. The English version was reprinted many times on both sides of the Atlantic and elsewhere in the English-speaking world. It was still in print in the 1980s and is currently being made available online.

6. Significant connections between theological anti-Judaism and "racial" antisemitism, however, are argued, for example, in Uriel Tal, *Religious and Anti-religious Roots of Modern Anti-Semitism* (1971), and Rosemary Radford Reuther, *Faith and Fratricide: The Theological Roots of Anti-Semitism* (1974). In addition, the prevalent insistence that Nazi leaders and followers were fundamentally anti-Christian is simply not borne out by the historical evidence, as has now been overwhelmingly shown by the groundbreaking research of Richard Steigmann-Gall, *The Holy Reich: Nazi Conceptions of Christianity* (2003): though the Nazis were anticlerical, they were on the whole very much in favor of a developed Christianity, which they claimed had been started up by a non-Jewish Jesus.

7. "Classical Music, Concerts in Town," *New Yorker*, 25 December 2006.

8. That is, as governed by the use of Psalm 2 in the New Testament at Acts 4:25,27.

9. Several significant examples include the following: Genesis 48:19, "[Jacob-cum-Israel's grandson Ephraim's] offspring will become a multitude of the nations [*melo ha-goyim*]"; Genesis 25:23, "And the LORD said to her [Rebekah, who was pregnant with twins], 'Two nations [*goyim*] are in your womb, and . . . the elder [Esau, father of the nation of the Edomites] shall serve the younger [Jacob, father of the nation of the Israelites]'"; and Exodus 19:6, "You [the Israelites] shall be for me [the LORD God] a priestly kingdom and a holy nation [a *goy kadosh*]"; see also, however, Numbers 23:9.

10. Earlier in this number the text says of the Daughter of Sion (Jerusalem), "behold thy King cometh unto thee." Traditional Christianity understands the "daughter" to be Christians, not Jewish unbelievers in Jesus. The phrases "Zion" and "(heavenly) Jerusalem" were adopted for the church, the place where God dwells—see Hebrews 12:22, Revelation 14:1—now that the Lord God had apparently rejected the Temple (at Mount Zion) and the earthly Jerusalem.

11. Note that this heightening can hold true whether or not it was Jennens's main purpose in emending the English biblical text.

12. It's worth noting here that the language of the adjoining verse (Malachi 3:4) is repeated often in traditional Jewish liturgy, to this day, as an expression of hope about the restoration of appropriate worship in a future,

third Temple. The Jewish liturgy of Handel's day is discussed in detail in Gamaliel ben Pedahzur, *The Book of Religion, Ceremonies, and Prayers of the Jews* (1738).

13. As, for example, in the following sermons: Isaac Barrow, "That Jesus is the true Messias" (1716); Samuel Clarke, "On the Fullness of Time in which Christ appeared" (1730); John Kettlewell, "That Jesus Is the Christ, from Ancient Prophecies" (1719); and John Tillotson, "The Presence of the Messias, the Glory of the Second Temple" (1728).

14. Jennens owned two paintings depicting this scene of Melchizedek and Abraham, according to Thomas Martyn, *The English Connoisseur: Containing an Account of Whatever is curious in Painting, Sculpture, &c. in the Palaces and Seats of the Nobility and Principal Gentry of England* (1766).

15. It's perhaps worth noting that Psalm 2 had a long-standing liturgical use in connection with the doctrine of the incarnation (i.e., according to which God took on human form in Jesus). For example, the traditional Introit of the First Mass of the Feast of the Nativity, *Dominus dixit ad me: filius meus es tu, ego hodie genui* [Psalm 2:7], quotes 2:1, "Quare fremuerunt gentes: et populi meditati sunt inania?"

The choice was probably also conditioned by the quotation of Psalm 2 in the New Testament at Acts 4:25–28, as 4:27 includes the reference to God's "holy child/servant," Jesus. The unspoken, but nevertheless clearly implied, message was that Jesus "came unto his own [i.e., Old Israel, "the Jews"—see also Exodus 19:5], and his own received him not" (John 1:11).

16. For an extremely similar rage aria, see the opening movement from the motet *Barbara, dira, effera Hebreae gentis rabies!* by Handel's contemporary Jan Dismas Zelenka (1679–1745), the text of which reads: "Barbarous, horrible, and wild [was] the savageness of the Hebrew nation, who confounded the holy cross [of Jesus] with the crosses of the thieves! . . . Your barbarity has been overcome and now lies groaning. . . . Savageness has been tamed. . . . Victory, applaud Christ for all his many triumphs. Allelujah." (Note that the motet's text has been bowdlerized in prominent modern performances, such as by the group Musica Antiqua Köln, to *Barbara, dira, effera immanes gentis rabies!*, and given in translation as: "The ferocious, fierce, and terrible fury of the brutal people.")

17. It's also interesting to note that wording from Psalm 2 (specifically Psalm 2:1) is employed in connection with the destruction of the Jerusalem Temple for several kinot (laments) that have been included from the Middle Ages to the present in Judaism's morning service of Tishah B'Av (e.g., at line 39 of kinah 16 and line 39 of kinah 18 in Avrohom Chaim Feuer and Avie Gold, *The Complete Tishah B'Av Service* [2003]).

18. It's, admittedly, unclear whether Newton means that only believers in Jesus are both holy and fully in possession of the faculty of understanding (he's not likely to be saying that Christians are "smart" and Jews are "stupid"), or simply that unbelievers in Jesus will have utterly perished by this point and therefore be unable to exercise their intellects.

19. Readers may be interested to know that Vespasian and Titus are immortalized on the first-century Arch of Titus, located on the Via Sacra in Rome. This arch commemorates the destruction of Jerusalem in the war of 66–73 CE. Significantly, the Arch of Titus served as the general model for many later arches of triumph, the most familiar of which is the Arc de Triomphe in Paris. One of the panels from the Arch of Titus portrays the Romans having made off with various treasures from the Jerusalem Temple, notably a large menorah (one of the three main furnishings of the Temple), thus leading to this arch's becoming a symbol of the Jewish Diaspora (until the establishing of the State of Israel, in 1948). In the Middle Ages, Jews would not walk under the Arch of Titus. Pope Paul IV (1476–1559), however, who ghettoized Rome's Jews, forced them to swear an annual oath of submission at this site.

20. Compare "the nation [*ethnos*] of the Jews" at Acts 10:22; the various references to "the Jews" as a "nation [*ethnos*]" at John 11 and 18; and, likewise, the prediction that "[Jacob-cum-Israel's grandson Ephraim's] offspring ['the Jews'] will become a multitude of the nations [Hebrew, *melo ha-goyim*]" at Genesis 48:19.

21. Strictly speaking, the final volume of Henry's *Exposition*, which covers the books of Romans to Revelation, was not written by Henry himself. Rather, after his death a group of (historicist) ministers anonymously completed the series, working from notes on his expounding of Scripture taken by "some of the Relations and Hearers of that excellent Person." The question of authorship doesn't materially affect the points I'm making here.

22. At "Glory to God in the highest," no. 17 in the libretto, trumpets are used (without drums), but they are instructed to play *da lontano e un poco piano* ("softly and at a distance"). Some performances today do include trumpets and drums earlier on in *Messiah*, but these rely on new orchestrations devised after Handel's death.

23. John H. Roberts, "False *Messiah*," *Journal of the American Musicological Society* (2010).

24. Burney, *An Account of the Musical Performances in Westminster-Abbey*, writes of this theme from the *Israel in Egypt* chorus: "The [melodic] intervals in this counter-subject are exactly the same as in the celebrated canon *Non Nobis Domine*. Whether the subject occurred to HANDEL accidentally, or was taken with design, I know not; . . . As to the *original*

inventor, or *right owner* of that series of notes upon which the canon, which tradition has given to Bird [i.e., William Byrd, c. 1540–1623], was constructed, they had been the subject of fugue to [Gioseffo] Zarlino [1517–90], and to old Adrian Villaert [c. 1490–1562], his master, long before Bird was born; and, indeed, constitute one of the different species of *tetrachord,* used by the Greeks, in the highest antiquity." (*Tetrachord* means "four [lyre] strings," signifying a series of four incrementally higher pitches such that the lengths of the shortest and longest strings are in a three-to-four ratio; the modern "major scale" can be divided into two instances of the particular species of tetrachord found in the Byrd canon: do-re-mi-fa and sol-la-ti-do.) In discussing the Hallelujah chorus, however, Burney makes no reference to *Non Nobis Domine.*

25. There are instances of striking musical similarities that do have to be deemed coincidental. For example, in no. 12 ("Death") from *The First Part of Ayres, French, Pollish and others together . . . with Pavines, Galliards, and Almaines* (1605) of the obscure composer Captain Tobias Hume (1579–1645), the melody at times sounds startlingly like a rather distinctive twelve-note melodic and rhythmic idea found in Herman Hupfeld's 1931 song "As Time Goes By," made famous in 1942 when it was performed by the character Sam in the movie *Casablanca.* Hupfeld can of course hardly be quoting Captain Hume.

26. Among the best known of these sculptures is the representation of triumphant Ecclesia with Wise Virgins and abject Synagoga with Foolish Virgins at the Erfurt Cathedral. Depictions of similarly abject Synagoga are also found in prominent modern art. See, e.g., John Singer Sargent, *Synagogue,* from his cycle *Triumph of Religion—A Mural Decoration Illustrating Certain Stages of Jewish and Christian Religious History* (third-floor staircase hall of the Boston Public Library). Judaism's personification is here pictured as an aged muscular female, gripping the upright and unbroken tablets of Law. She is blindfolded, however, and her crown is toppled and her staff broken; furthermore, she is shrouded in the torn veil of the Jerusalem Temple.

27. See now Robert P. Ericksen, *Complicity in the Holocaust: Churches and Universities in Nazi Germany* (2012).

28. The key word here is *katakauchō.* Biblical-Greek dictionaries define the word as "to boast in triumphant comparison with others," "to glory against," "to exult over," "to boast one's self to the injury of," and "to rejoice against." *Katakauchō* is used also at James 2:13, which the King James Bible gives as "For he shall have judgment without mercy, that hath shewed no mercy; and mercy *rejoiceth against* judgment." Romans 11:17–18 served as the epigraph also for Marissen, "Rejoicing against Judaism in Handel's *Messiah,*" *Journal of Musicology* (2007).

29. This would speak to the interpretive question of whether Jennens and Handel, in their day, could and should in principle "have known better" than to express any Christian rejoicing against Judaism (see, e.g., Peter Kivy, "*Messiah*'s Message: Con or Anti," in his *Sounding Off* [2012]). Several doors of egress have been seriously suggested to me by prominent intellectuals: one can insist that *Messiah* is not in fact triumphalistically anti-Judaic, and so consideration of Romans 11 would be altogether irrelevant; one can argue that any rejoicing against Judaism in *Messiah* is real but surely represents sheer oblivious blunder on Jennens and Handel's part, whose intentions regarding Judaism in *Messiah* will have been neutral at worst; or one can contend that Jennens and Handel may well have had triumphalistic anti-Judaic intentions in mind for *Messiah* but were unsuccessful in realizing them.

30. Compare also Warburton's comments in the prefatory material from his *Divine Legation of Moses*, first published in 1738–41: "The *New Testament* . . . makes *Judaism* the great Foundation of *Christianity*. . . . Right Reason, as well as St. *Paul* (which with us [Christians], at present, are the same Thing) would teach . . . , *Boast not against the Branches of the natural Olive-tree*."

31. Consider the severity, for example, at John 8:23–47, "[Jesus] said to them ['the Jews' who had not abided in his word], 'You are from below, I am from above . . . but now you seek to kill me, a man who has told you the truth which I heard from God; . . . If God were your father, you would love me. . . . Why do you not understand what I say? It is because you cannot bear to hear my word. You are of your father the devil, and your will is to do your father's desires. He was a murderer from the beginning, and has nothing to do with the truth, because there is no truth in him. When he lies, he speaks according to his own nature, for he is a liar and the father of lies. . . . He who is of God hears the words of God; the reason why you do not hear them is that *you* ['the Jews'] *are not of God*.'" (The particular historical community out of which the Gospel of John was produced is said at John 9:22, 12:42, and 16:2 to have had its members who proclaimed belief in Jesus as God's messiah excluded from the synagogue.) Note, however, that nowhere, even at its most severe, does the Gospel of John *rejoice* against Judaism.

32. In *Jesus & Israel: One Covenant or Two?* (1995), the biblical scholar and theologian David E. Holwerda writes: "I hold with the apostle Paul [see Romans 9–11, especially the plain sense of 11:26a (but as opposed to the plain sense of John 3:18b?)] that the category of election still applies to the Jewish people, even those who do not now believe in Jesus." A Christian belief that post-Jesus Jews are not God's people has fueled much anti-Jewish sentiment and violent action; for a history, see James Carroll, *Constantine's Sword: The Church and the Jews* (2001).

33. Several recent publications on *Messiah* do not reckon with the import of this directive of Paul's about Judaism in Romans 11 (for the reason that they don't think it is relevant to the Hallelujah chorus). See Ben Finane, *Handel's Messiah and His English Oratorios* (2009); Calvin Stapert, *Handel's Messiah: Comfort for God's People* (2010); Roberts, "False *Messiah*" (2010 and 2011); and Kivy, "*Messiah*'s Message" (2012). The title of Stapert's biblically oriented study faces the now-prickly theological problem of suggesting that today's Jews who don't believe in Jesus are not God's people—since Jews can't experience the comforts that Stapert's book discusses unless they become Christians, it would follow from the title of his book that the category of election does not apply to the Jewish people as a whole.

34. In today's German-language hymnals, the second line typically reads "Und steure deine Feinde Mord" ("and restrain the murderousness of your enemies").

35. In today's English-language hymnals, the first stanza typically reads: "Lord, keep us steadfast in your word; / Curb those who by deceit or sword / Would wrest the kingdom from your Son / And bring to naught all he has done."

36. Compare this excerpt from the Good Friday liturgy in the *Book of Common Prayer*: "O Merciful God, who hast made all men, and hatest nothing that thou hast made, nor wouldest the death of a sinner, but rather that he should be converted and live; Have mercy upon all Jews, Turks, Infidels, and Hereticks, and take from them all ignorance, hardness of heart, and contempt of thy word; and so fetch them home, blessed Lord, to thy flock, that they may be saved among the remnant of the true Israelites, and be made one fold under one Shepherd, Jesus Christ our Lord, who liveth and reigneth with thee and the holy Spirit, one God, world without end. Amen."

37. This isn't to suggest that the text of 1 Peter 2:24–25 (drawing on Isaiah 53:5–6) is saying that the rest of the world does not consist of people who could be potential believers in Jesus and be "healed." My point is that the author of 1 Peter 2 is explicitly speaking to "you which believe"—*Christians*, not Jewish or pagan unbelievers in Jesus. So when *Messiah* says (prophetically quoting Isaiah 53), "with his stripes *we* are healed" and "all *we*, like sheep, have gone astray," the *we* is referring to Christians; and when, however, *Messiah* says "all *they* that see him, laugh him to scorn," the *they* is referring to Jewish unbelievers in Jesus.

38. An earlier reading here of several words is crossed out, apparently by Jennens, and is now illegible.

39. See, for example, the mention of the scriptures from ancient Israel being divided into "the Law and the Prophets" at Romans 3:21, Matthew 5:17, Luke 16:16, Acts 28:23, and John 1:45.

40. See the mention of the Scriptures from ancient Israel being divided into "the Law," "the Prophets," and "the Psalms" at Luke 24:44. This is close to the threefold division of Scripture traditionally maintained in Judaism: the Torah, the Prophets, and the Writings.

41. Consider the printing in England of *The Traditions of the Jews, with the Expositions and Doctrines of the Rabbins Contain'd in the Talmud and Other Rabbinical Writings*, an abridged translation—issued in 1732–34 and reissued in 1742–43 and 1748—of Johann Andreas Eisenmenger's notorious book, *Entdecktes Judenthum* (which translates as "Judaism unmasked") of 1711.

42. The original instance of an eighteenth-century aristocrat—a leading Handel scholar, Donald Burrows (*Handel: Messiah* [1995]), has shown it most probably was *not* the king—standing for the Hallelujah chorus (which may have been not for *Messiah* but for the reuse of this chorus in the very different context of Handel's *Foundling Anthem*) is much debated. Whatever this event was, of course, others at the event would then have been required, for reasons of social etiquette, to stand too. We don't know for certain what caused that aristocrat to stand up. The following, however, is the historical source suggesting the proud English origins (and perhaps also the cause?) of the tradition. A late-eighteenth-century report, in a letter of James Beattie to Revd Dr Laing, says: "When Messiah was first performed, the audience was exceedingly struck and affected by the music in general; but when that chorus struck up, 'For the Lord God Omnipotent reigneth [within the Hallelujah chorus],' they were so transported that they all, together with the king (who happened to be present), *started* up, and remained standing till the chorus ended: and hence it became the fashion in England for the audience to stand while that part of the music is performing. [*This*] *does great honour . . . to the English nation*" (my italics). Audiences were not in any sense bound to stand up for *subsequent* performances of the Hallelujah chorus (i.e., ones in which the king or other such aristocrat wasn't around to stand and thereby force them, as it were, to stand up too). We don't know for certain what the actual cause of this tradition of standing for *Messiah* is. Presumably to the extent that modern audiences think about it at all, they would suppose that standing reflected an approbation by the king or aristocrat of the Hallelujah chorus, and they would further suppose that approval by standing is a worthy practice for all performances of this chorus.

A notion that standing for the chorus celebrated only what might be called a "pure" *aesthetic* judgment of "the music itself" strikes me (pace Kivy, "*Messiah*'s Message: Con or Anti?" [2012]) as naive in the extreme. Surely celebration also of the triumphal biblical text will have played a role, whether or not in *Messiah* the particular arrangement of words and their magnificent musical setting would ever have been understood as specifically anti-Judaic.

III. THE *MESSIAH* LIBRETTO

1. In light of the other historical references in the book of Daniel, though, the "anointed leader" of verse 25 may be a prophetic reference to Zerubbabel (a descendant of the Davidic family) or to the high priest Joshua ben Josadak (see, e.g., Zechariah 6:11), and the "anointed one" of verse 26 apparently most probably prophesies the high priest Onias III (see Maccabees 4:30–34).

2. Some will cite Daniel 9:26 as a prophecy of God's suffering messiah. The meaning of the Hebrew text here, however, is uncertain and contested (and in any event, as mentioned earlier, this prophecy apparently most probably applies to Onias III). The KJV renders the passage: "And after threescore and two weeks shall Messiah be cut off, but not for himself"; the Douay-Rheims Bible: "And after sixty-two weeks Christ shall be slain: and the people that shall deny him shall not be his"; the New International Version: "After the sixty-two 'sevens,' the Anointed One will be cut off and will have nothing"; and the Jewish Publication Society Tanakh: "And after those sixty-two weeks, the anointed one will disappear and vanish." It may also be worth noting that, so far as anyone knows, no pre- or non-Christian Jewish texts saw Daniel 9:26 as predicting the suffering and violent death of God's messiah.

3. As encouraged, to be sure, by Luke 24:25–26, where, on the Sunday after his crucifixion, the resurrected Jesus says to Cleopas and another of his grieving followers (who don't recognize that it is Jesus before them), "O how foolheaded you are, and how slow of heart to believe all that the prophets have said! Was it not necessary that the messiah should suffer these things and then enter into his glory?" (Greek: . . . *ouchi tauta edei pathein ton christon*).

4. This wouldn't have had to be "after the fact," says Boyarin, *The Jewish Gospels* (2012), who argues that there was nothing at all un-Jewish about any aspect of the New Testament depiction of Jesus as God's messiah—thus all the elements that have been customarily understood by Jews and Christians as marking a Christian break with Jewish messianic beliefs may well have been included among the expectations of at least some pre-Jesus Jews.

5. A recitative setting of this text survives, which, if composed by Handel, may have been performed in 1742.

6. See Jennens and Handel's next number for a contrasting "all *they*."

7. See Jennens and Handel's previous number for a contrasting "all *we*."

8. An eighteenth-century setting of this text as a recitative survives, but its composer is thought not to be Handel.

BIBLIOGRAPHICAL NOTE

In addition to the marvelous book of Tassilo Erhardt's, listed in the Works Cited, I found the following studies on Jennens and Handel to be most helpful in my learning about *Messiah*, though I don't necessarily quote from these sources in my work:

Ruth Smith's revelatory study *Handel's Oratorios and Eighteenth-Century Thought* (1995) provides essential reading on the history of ideas. Also extremely important is her article "The Achievements of Charles Jennens," *Music and Letters* (1989).

An additional valuable study on Jennens is Brenda Sumner's "Gopsall Hall: 'Look on my works, ye Mighty, and despair,'" MA thesis, University of Leicester (2009).

Hamish Swanston's *Handel* (1990) offers a remarkably insightful delineation of contemporaneous theological currents.

Richard Luckett's *Handel's Messiah: A Celebration* (1992) delivers an enlightening cultural and social biography of Handel's work.

And Donald Burrows's *Handel: Messiah* (1995) makes available an indispensable compendium of textual and musicological information.

Finally, a great deal of important historical information is provided in the regrettably often overlooked or unheeded essay, David Hunter, "George Frideric Handel and the Jews: Fact, Fiction, and the Tolerances of Scholarship," in *For the Love of Music: Festschrift in Honor of Theodore Front on His 90th Birthday* (2002). Hunter's essay takes note, too, of the transparent anti-Judaism in Handel's oratorio *La resurrezione*. On the anti-Judaism in Handel's passion oratorio *Der für die Sünde der Welt gemartete und sterbende Jesus* ("Brockes-Passion"), see Marissen, *Lutheranism, Anti-Judaism, and Bach's St. John Passion* (1998). For more on theological anti-Judaism in baroque music, see Marissen, "The Character and Sources of the

Anti-Judaism in Bach's Cantata 46," *Harvard Theological Review* (2003); and the other items by Marissen in the Works Cited.

❖ ❖ ❖

For a formidable, somber presentation of the long and troubling history of Jew hatred in England, from the Middle Ages to this day, see Anthony Julius, *Trials of the Diaspora: A History of Anti-Semitism in England* (2010).

And for an accessible and extremely informative introduction to the New Testament's history, textual criticism, theology, and anti-Judaism, see Bart D. Ehrman, *Jesus, Interrupted: Revealing the Hidden Contradictions in the Bible (and Why We Don't Know about Them)* (2009); likewise Amy-Jill Levine, *The Misunderstood Jew: The Church and the Scandal of the Jewish Jesus* (2006).

A most useful reference work is Edward Kessler and Neil Wenborn, eds., *A Dictionary of Jewish-Christian Relations* (2005); likewise, Amy-Jill Levine and Marc Zvi Brettler, eds., *The Jewish Annotated New Testament* (2011).

In my reading of the apostle Paul, I've been heavily influenced by Stanley K. Stowers, *A Rereading of Romans: Justice, Jews, and Gentiles* (1994); Krister Stendahl, *Final Account: Paul's Letter to the Romans* (1995); and Dale B. Martin, *The Corinthian Body* (1995).

For a trenchant reading of the King James Bible, see Harold Bloom, *The Shadow of a Great Rock: A Literary Appreciation of the King James Bible* (2011).

Ruth HaCohen has traced the tensions between Jewish "noise" and idealized Christian "harmony" and their artistic manifestations all the way from the high Middle Ages to Nazi Germany in her extremely significant and important book *The Music Libel against the Jews* (2011).

WORKS CITED

1. SEVENTEENTH- AND EIGHTEENTH-CENTURY LITERATURE

Items marked with an asterisk are specifically known to have been owned by Charles Jennens, the librettist for Handel's *Messiah*, mostly either as documented in the magnificent book by Tassilo Erhardt, listed in section 2, or as documented by the items' printed subscriber lists that I've uncovered. Many of the seventeenth- and eighteenth-century books cited here were also reprinted in subsequent centuries.

Antony Alsop, *Messiah: A Christmas Song* (pre-1715).

Anonymous, *A Paraphrase and Exposition of the Book of Psalms; Designed Principally for the Use of the Unlearned Reader* (1768).

*Isaac Barrow, "Of the Imperfection of the Jewish Religion," in *The Works of the learned Isaac Barrow . . . Sermons and Expositions upon all the Articles in The Apostles Creed* (1716).

*———, "That Jesus is the true Messias," in *The Works of the learned Isaac Barrow . . . Sermons and Expositions upon all the Articles in The Apostles Creed* (1716).

*Sir Richard Blackmore, *A Paraphrase on the Book of Job as likewise on the Songs of Moses, Deborah, David, on four select Psalms, some Chapters of Isaiah, and the Third Chapter of Habakkuk* (1700).

The Book of Common Prayer, and Administration of the Sacraments, and other Rites and Ceremonies of the Church, according to the Use of the Church of England; together with the Psalter or Psalms of David, pointed as They are to be Sung or Said in Churches (1728).

The Book of Common Prayer, and Administration of the Sacraments; and Other Rites and Ceremonies of the Church of England; with the Psalter, or Psalms of David (1638).

James Boswell, *Life of Samuel Johnson* (1791).

*John Boswell, *A Method of Study; or, An useful Library . . . Containing some Directions for the Study of Divinity* (1738–43).

*Robert Boyle, *The Works of the Honourable Robert Boyle* (1744).

Charles Burney, *An Account of the Musical Performances in Westminster-Abbey, and the Pantheon . . . 1784: In Commemoration of Handel* (1785).

Edward Chandler, *A Defence of Christianity, from the Prophecies of the Old Testament* (1725).

*Samuel Clarke, "On the Fullness of Time in which Christ appeared," in his *Sermons on the Following Subjects, viz. . . . The Prediction of the MESSIAH, The Character of the MESSIAH . . . Of the Spiritual Nature of the Gospel* (1730).

———, *A Paraphrase on the Four Evangelists . . . Very useful for Families* (1736).

*Samuel Davies, *Sermons on the most useful and important Subjects, adapted to the Family and Closet* (1766).

Thomas Deacon, *A Compleat Collection of Devotions, both Publick and Private; taken from the Apostolical Constitutions, the Ancient Liturgies, and the Common Prayer Book of the Church of England* (1734).

*Philip Doddridge, *The Family Expositor; or, A Paraphrase and Version of the New Testament; with Critical Notes* (1739–56).

Johann Andreas Eisenmenger, *Entdecktes Judenthum* (1711).

———, *The Traditions of the Jews, with the Expositions and Doctrines of the Rabbins contain'd in the Talmud and other Rabbinical Writings*, trans. John Peter Stehelin (1732–34).

Thomas Fenton, *Annotations on the Book of Job, and the Psalms; Collected from several Commentators, and Methodized and Improved* (1732).

Henry Hammond, *A Paraphrase and Annotations upon all the Books of the New Testament, Briefly Explaining all the Difficult Places Thereof* (1653).

———, *A Paraphrase and Annotations upon the Books of the Psalms, Briefly Explaining the Difficulties Thereof* (1659).

Matthew Henry, *An Exposition of all the Books of the Old and New Testament: . . . with Practical Remarks and Observations* (1721–25).

Samuel Humphreys, *The Sacred Books of the Old and New Testament, Recited at Large and Illustrated with Critical and Explanatory Annotations, Carefully Compiled from the Commentaries and other Writings of . . . Eminent Authors, Ancient and Modern* (1735–39).

*Jennens-Holdsworth correspondence, 1729–46; original documents, housed at the Gerald Coke Handel Collection of the Foundling

Museum in London, there described as: "Comprising: Forty holograph letters from Charles Jennens to Edward Holdsworth / Seventy-one letters from Holdsworth to Jennens / Receipt by Jennens signed by Paul Vaillant with a note and contract / Two letters from Lord Digby to Jennens / Drafts of Jennens' obituary for Holdsworth and his inscription for the monument built at Gopsall / Seven letters from Henry Holdsworth to Jennens."

*John Kettlewell, "That Jesus is the Christ, from Ancient Prophecies," in his *A Compleat Collection of the Works of the Reverend and learned John Kettlewell* (1719).

*Richard Kidder, *A Demonstration of the Messias, in Which the Truth of the Christian Religion Is Proved, Against All the Enemies Thereof; but Especially Against the Jews* (1726).

———, "That Part of Bishop Kidder's Demonstration of the Messias, Preach'd at Boyle's Lectures, Abridg'd," in Gilbert Burnet, ed., *A Defence of Natural and Revealed Religion: Being an Abridgment of the Sermons preached at the Lecture founded by the Honble Robert Boyle, Esq;* (1737).

George Lavington, *The Nature and Use of a Type* (1724).

Lyra Davidica (1708).

Thomas Martyn, *The English Connoisseur: Containing an Account of Whatever is curious in Painting, Sculpture, &c. in the Palaces and Seats of the Nobility and Principal Gentry of England* (1766).

John Newton, *Messiah: Fifty Expository Discourses, on the Series of Scriptural Passages, which form the Subject of the Celebrated Oratorio of Handel—Preached in the years 1784 and 1785, in the Parish Church of St. Mary Woolnoth* (1786).

*William Nicholls, *Commentary on the Book of Common-Prayer* (1712).

*John Pearson, *An Exposition of the Creed* (1710).

Gamaliel ben Pedahzur, *The Book of Religion, Ceremonies, and Prayers of the Jews* (1738).

*Edward Pococke, *Commentaries on Hosea, Joel, Micah, and Malachi* (1740).

Psalmodia Germanica; or, The German Psalmody (1732).

*Robert South, "Jesus of Nazareth Proved the True and Only Promised Messiah," in his *Sermons Preached upon Several Occasions* (1737).

Thomas Sternhold and John Hopkins, *The Whole Book of Psalms: collected into English Metre* (1730).

*John Tillotson, "The Presence of the Messias, the Glory of the Second Temple," in his *The Works of the Most Reverend Dr. John Tillotson . . . containing Fifty Four Sermons and Discourses, On Several Occasions* (1728).

*Joseph Trapp, *The Works of Virgil; translated into Blank Verse, with Large Explanatory Notes, and Critical Observations* (1731).
*William Warburton, *The Divine Legation of Moses Demonstrated, in Nine Books* (1766).
Isaac Watts, *Songs Attempted in Easy Language for the Use of Children* (1735).
*Edward Wells, *An Help for the More Easy and Clear Understanding of the Holy Scriptures: being all the Epistles of St Paul* (1715).
*———, *An Help for the More Easy and Clear Understanding of the Holy Scriptures: being St Paul's two Epistles to the Corinthians* (1714).
*———, *An Help for the More Easy and Clear Understanding of the Holy Scriptures: being the Books of Isaiah, Jeremiah, and Lamentations* (1728).
*———, *An Help for the More Easy and Clear Understanding of the Holy Scriptures: being the Books of Job, Psalms, Proverbs, Ecclesiastes and Canticles* (1727).
*———, *An Help for the More Easy and Clear Understanding of the Holy Scriptures: being the Gospel of St John* (1719).
*———, *An Help for the More Easy and Clear Understanding of the Holy Scriptures: being the Revelation of St John the Divine* (1717).
*———. *An Help for the More Easy and Clear Understanding of the Holy Scriptures: being the Twelve Lesser Prophets* (1723).
*———. *An Help for the More Easy and Clear Understanding of the Holy Scriptures: being the two Gospels of St Matthew and St Mark* (1717).
*Daniel Whitby, *A Paraphrase and Commentary on the New Testament* (1718).

2. POST-EIGHTEENTH-CENTURY LITERATURE

Harold Bloom, *The Shadow of a Great Rock: A Literary Appreciation of the King James Bible* (New Haven, CT: Yale University Press, 2011).
John Bluck, *The Giveaway God: Ecumenical Bible Studies on Divine Generosity* (Geneva: World Council of Churches Publications, 2001).
Daniel Boyarin, *The Jewish Gospels: The Story of the Jewish Christ* (New York: New Press, 2012).
Donald Burrows, *Handel: Messiah* (Cambridge: Cambridge University Press, 1995).
James Carroll, *Constantine's Sword: The Church and the Jews* (Boston: Houghton Mifflin, 2001).
Arthur Danto, "The Space of Beauty," *New Republic*, 15 November 1982, 32–35.

Bart D. Ehrman, *Jesus, Interrupted: Revealing the Hidden Contradictions in the Bible (and Why We Don't Know about Them)* (New York: HarperOne, 2009).

Richard Eldridge, *An Introduction to the Philosophy of Art* (Cambridge: Cambridge University Press, 2003).

Todd M. Endelman, *The Jews of Georgian England, 1714–1830* (Philadelphia: Jewish Publication Society of America, 1979).

Tassilo Erhardt, "Rekonstruktion von Charles Jennens' theologischer Bibliothek," in his *Händels Messiah: Text, Musik, Theologie* (Bad Reichenhall, Germany: Comes-Verlag, 2007).

Robert P. Ericksen, *Complicity in the Holocaust: Churches and Universities in Nazi Germany* (Cambridge: Cambridge University Press, 2012).

Avrohom Chaim Feuer and Avie Gold, *The Complete Tishah B'Av Service: A New Translation and Anthologized Commentary* (Brooklyn, NY: Mesorah Publications, 2003).

Ben Finane, *Handel's Messiah and His English Oratorios* (New York: Continuum, 2009).

Ruth HaCohen, *The Music Libel against the Jews* (New Haven, CT: Yale University Press, 2011).

Ernst Wilhelm Hengstenberg, *Christologie des Alten Testaments und Commentar über die messianischen Weissagungen der Propheten* (Berlin: Oehmigke, 1829–35; 2nd ed., 1854–57); English translation by Reuel Kieth: *Christology of the Old Testament, and a Commentary on the Predictions of the Messiah by the Prophets* (Alexandria, VA: Morrison, 1836–39; trans. of 2nd ed., by Theodore Meyer and James Martin, Edinburgh: T. & T. Clark, 1854–65).

David E. Holwerda, *Jesus & Israel: One Covenant or Two?* (Grand Rapids, MI: Eerdmans, 1995).

David Hunter, "George Frideric Handel and the Jews: Fact, Fiction, and the Tolerances of Scholarship," in Darwin F. Scott, ed., *For the Love of Music: Festschrift in Honor of Theodore Front on His 90th Birthday*, 5–28 (Lucca, Italy: Lim Antiqua, 2002).

Donald Juel, *Messianic Exegesis: Christological Interpretation of the Old Testament in Early Christianity* (Minneapolis: Fortress Press, 1988).

Anthony Julius, *Trials of the Diaspora: A History of Anti-Semitism in England* (New York: Oxford University Press, 2010).

Edward Kessler and Neil Wenborn, eds., *A Dictionary of Jewish-Christian Relations* (Cambridge: Cambridge University Press, 2005).

Peter Kivy, "*Messiah*'s Message: Con or Anti," in his *Sounding Off: Eleven Essays in the Philosophy of Music* (New York: Oxford University Press, 2012).

Berel Lang, "On the 'the' in 'the Jews': or, From Grammar to Antisemitism," *Midstream* 49, no. 4 (2003): 9–11.

Amy-Jill Levine, *The Misunderstood Jew: The Church and the Scandal of the Jewish Jesus* (New York: HarperOne, 2006).

Amy-Jill Levine and Marc Zvi Brettler, eds., *The Jewish Annotated New Testament* (New York: Oxford University Press, 2011).

Richard Luckett, *Handel's Messiah: A Celebration* (London: V. Gollancz, 1992).

Michael Marissen, *Bach's Oratorios—The Parallel German-English Texts, with Annotations* (New York: Oxford University Press, 2008).

———, "Blood, People, and Crowds in Matthew, Luther, and Bach," *Lutheran Quarterly* 19 (2005): 1–22; excerpted in *Luther Digest: An Annual Abridgement of Luther Studies* 16 (2008): 43–45.

———, "The Character and Sources of the Anti-Judaism in Bach's Cantata 46," *Harvard Theological Review* 96 (2003): 63–99.

———, "Communication [regarding John H. Roberts's article, 'False Messiah']," *Journal of the American Musicological Society* 64 (2011): 471–78.

———, *Lutheranism, Anti-Judaism, and Bach's St. John Passion* (New York: Oxford University Press, 1998).

———, "Rejoicing against Judaism in Handel's *Messiah*," *Journal of Musicology* 24 (2007): 167–94.

Dale B. Martin, *The Corinthian Body* (New Haven, CT: Yale University Press, 1995).

Harold Pollins, *Economic History of the Jews in England* (London: Associated University Presses, 1982).

Rosemary Radford Reuther, *Faith and Fratricide: The Theological Roots of Anti-Semitism* (New York: Seabury Press, 1974).

John H. Roberts, "False *Messiah*," *Journal of the American Musicological Society* 63 (2010): 45–97; and 64 (2011): 478–81.

Ruth Smith, "The Achievements of Charles Jennens," *Music and Letters* 70 (1989): 161–90.

———, *Charles Jennens: The Man behind Handel's Messiah* (London: Handel House Trust and Gerald Coke Handel Foundation, 2012).

———, *Handel's Oratorios and Eighteenth-Century Thought* (Cambridge: Cambridge University Press, 1995).

Calvin Stapert, *Handel's Messiah: Comfort for God's People* (Grand Rapids, MI: Eerdmans, 2010).

Richard Steigmann-Gall, *The Holy Reich: Nazi Conceptions of Christianity, 1919–1945* (Cambridge: Cambridge University Press, 2003).

Krister Stendahl, *Final Account: Paul's Letter to the Romans* (Minneapolis: Fortress Press, 1995).

Stanley K. Stowers, *A Rereading of Romans: Justice, Jews, and Gentiles* (New Haven, CT: Yale University Press, 1994).

Brenda Sumner, "Gopsall Hall: 'Look on my works, ye Mighty, and despair,'" MA thesis, University of Leicester, United Kingdom, 2009.

Hamish Swanston, *Handel* (London: G. Chapman, 1990).

Uriel Tal, *Religious and Anti-Religious Roots of Modern Anti-Semitism— The Leo Baeck Memorial Lecture 14* (1971); also in his *Religion, Politics and Ideology in the Third Reich: Selected Essays* (London: Routledge, 2004).

Herbert Weinstock, *Handel* (New York: Alfred A. Knopf, 1946).

INDEX OF MOVEMENTS FROM HANDEL'S *MESSIAH*

INDEX OF BIBLICAL SOURCES

INDEX OF NAMES AND SUBJECTS